D1686078

The international grain trade

The international grain trade

MICHAEL ATKIN

WOODHEAD PUBLISHING LIMITED
Cambridge, England

Published by Woodhead Publishing Ltd, Abington Hall, Abington, Cambridge CB1 6AH, England

First published 1992, Woodhead Publishing Ltd

British Library Cataloguing in Publication Data
A catalogue record for this book is available from the British Library.

ISBN 1 85573 068 5

Designed by Andrew Jones (text) and Chris Feely (jacket),
typeset by BookEns Ltd, Baldock, Herts. and printed by St Edmundsbury Press

Contents

Tables

Figures

Preface

The grain market has a powerful hold on the imagination. Grain has an importance shared by few other commodities, even though readers in industrialized countries may feel far removed from the bread riots, malnutrition and shortages that are so important in human history. On the other hand, it is traded and shipped around the world just like tea, oil or Deutsch Marks and, like other commodities, its price goes up and down, often rapidly and by large amounts. To those in the industry and to economists there is no paradox here, but the broader public may feel differently.

This book introduces the grain market to those who have not yet made its acquaintance. It is a fascinating market and I hope the reader will gain some insights into why it is so. It is also genuinely important for human welfare and for the global trading system. If this book helps to increase public understanding of how and why the grain market works as it does and the issues of public policy it raises, a useful purpose will have been served. A book of this size cannot cover every aspect of grain, but I hope it will be found to be a reasonably comprehensive introduction. It is designed to illustrate the political and economic dynamics of the world's grain trade, explaining how the industry works and analyzing its recent history. Wheat and the major coarse grains: maize (known as corn in the USA), rye, millet, barley, oats and grain sorghum will be the main focus of attention.

I have written this book in a personal capacity. It reflects only my own views and nothing in it should be attributed to the World Bank Group, its Board of Directors, its management or any of its member countries.

I have been studying and participating in the grain markets for many years and over these years I have accumulated far too many debts to acknowledge them all here and I certainly do not wish to imply that any of the views expressed herein are necessarily shared by any friends or colleagues. Without implicating them, I would like to thank all the people at the US Department of Agriculture who have answered scores of questions over the years and met countless requests for data, always speedily and always with good grace. My special thanks also to Winnie, for her understanding when writing this book took a lot of time from other things.

Michael Atkin

Author's note

Recent developments in (what used to be called) the Soviet Union have not given any comfort to those who hope for a rapid improvement in the country's agricultural production. The devolution of power from the centre to the republics is not likely to end the disarray in the agricultural marketing system, nor to improve the productivity of agricultural investment. In the short term, there is an increased likelihood of aid (particularly in the form of food) from the West, and there is some evidence that technical assistance for agricultural improvements is a priority of the international aid effort. Overall, however, nothing has happened to change the judgement made when the book was written: that dramatic improvements in production are a long way off, while the inevitable dislocations as a market economy is introduced will limit the ability of (whatever succeeds) the USSR to finance grain imports on a very large scale.

PART

I

Introduction

CHAPTER

1

Grain

Grains, or cereals, are the fruit of plants in the grass family. These relatively simple plants are the most important contributors to human nutrition. In developing countries, grains account for an estimated 60% of the calories and 55% of the protein in human diets.[1] In developed countries, people rely less on simple foods such as grains and get more of their nutrients from meat, fruit and vegetables. Yet grains are important indirectly, since they are used to feed the animals that produce meat, milk and eggs. Indeed, over half of the world's grain crop is fed to animals.

It is no wonder, therefore, that grains figure prominently in many crucial aspects of our society's economic and political affairs. On the one hand, there is the continuing presence of malnutrition and the threat of starvation in many countries. There are very few regions of the world where direct experience with serious food shortages or outright famine is not within living memory. Even in Western Europe there were deaths from starvation as recently as 1947. On the other hand there are agricultural surpluses in many rich countries, problems with farmers leaving the land because they cannot prosper in agriculture and serious disputes among nations over agricultural trade. The grain economy is rich with other ironies: under President Reagan,

1 These figures come from Raeburn, p16. Full details of all cited works can be found in the bibliography.

when the USA was building its military strength in an open arms race with the Soviet Union, the Cold War was at one of its most serious points and President Reagan's description of the USSR as an 'evil empire' seemed to encapsulate the hostility between the two superpowers, the Soviets were dependent on American grain to keep their people fed, and American farmers were dependent on Soviet purchases to provide a degree of support to grain prices. Indeed, one of Reagan's first actions after his election was to lift the embargo on grain sales to the USSR imposed by President Carter after the Soviet invasion of Afghanistan. Moreover, in 1987 and 1988 Reagan's government subsidized Soviet purchases of 13 million tonnes of grain, at a total bill to the US taxpayer of $447 million.[2]

Of course such ironies are perfectly understandable once one grasps the political and economic dynamics of the world's grain trade.

Grains and their role

Although the whole of the grain plant can be valuable, with the stalk reserved for straw or the entire plant cut and used for silage, it is the fruit, or seed, of the plant: i.e. the grain itself that will be the focus here. From this perspective, there are three important components of the grain. There is the husk, better known to consumers as bran; the endosperm, which consists essentially of carbohydrates (primarily starch), and the embryo, or 'germ', which is essentially protein. The protein content of grain varies widely; for most grains, between 50 and 140 g/kg (i.e. 5–14%) is crude protein, although there are some cultivars of wheat whose crude protein content is 220 g/kg. The quality of the protein is also variable, with the two amino acids lysine and methionine in particular being deficient in most grains.[3]

Grains therefore provide both protein and energy (carbohydrates) to the human and animal diet. Since the protein is not complete for humans, in traditionally vegetarian societies grain is supplemented with other, complementary vegetable proteins (such as beans). Grains and grain products (bread, for example) are normally thought of as sources of energy but they

2 This figure is based on an estimate of the average subsidy made by the US Department of Agriculture's (USDA) Economic Research Service. See United States General Accounting Office, *Agricultural Trade: Long Term Bilateral Grain Agreements with the Soviet Union and China*, p26.

3 Proteins are bundles of amino acids; 'complete' proteins are those that meet all the amino acid needs of the consumer; others lack certain amino acids.

are also important protein foods, and the difference between high-protein and low-protein grains will become important later.

Since the beginning of settled agriculture, grains have served a twin role in human nutrition. On the one hand, they provide human food directly (for example as bread). On the other hand, they are fed to animals who, in turn, provide meat, milk and eggs for human diets. A third use of grain, as a source of carbohydrate for processes such as distilling alcohol and producing starch, should also be noted, although it is small in quantitative terms.

A distinction is sometimes drawn between bread grains (wheat and rye) and the others; sometimes people will refer to feed grains and food grains, but since wheat is used both as a direct human food and as an animal feed, this is not a very helpful distinction. Most of this book will be spent discussing wheat and maize, since these two are both the most important in production, consumption and trade. It should be noted at the outset what is excluded. Rice is a grain, and it is very important in human diets in East and South Asia. It is excluded, however, because its patterns of production and trade are very different from those of the other grains, and a comprehensive treatment is not possible in a book of this size. There is also very limited substitutability, on either the production or consumption sides, between rice and other grains. (A brief discussion of the rice market is presented in the appendix.) Also excluded are soybeans as, although many people think of the soybean as a grain, it is in fact a legume. It is not covered in this book, however, not because of some slavish insistence on taxonomic purity, but to keep the text to manageable proportions. There are certainly important links between markets for grains and those for soybeans. On the supply side, in key producing regions farmers move land from maize to soybeans as relative prices change; on the demand side, the use of soybean meal (the main product of the soybean) as a protein feed for animals means there is a close relationship between it and grains in the animal feed market. To include soybeans along with the grains however would require treatment of soybean oil and, therefore, other oilseeds, and this would have led to a virtual doubling of the size of the book.

The grains concentrated on here are widely produced and consumed around the world, and are used in a great variety of applications. In order to understand the pattern of utilization, however, the mix of proteins and carbohydrates in grain needs to be discussed.

Proteins and carbohydrates

The nutritional needs of humans (and animals) are complex and diets need to be composed of several foods in order to be balanced. Of course, individual foodstuffs usually provide more than one nutrient, thus different combinations of foods can provide complete diets. Nutritional needs also vary with age, sex and workload. It is also crucial to remember that the market for foods is not simply driven by needs; a vitally important influence is taste.[4]

Carbohydrates

Carbohydrates are, chemically, the simplest of the major food groups, containing carbon, hydrogen and oxygen elements, and are derived from a great variety of foodstuffs. They provide energy in the diet. In the overall market for carbohydrates, grains compete with a wide range of other products. In the market for animal feed, this is particularly important: the range of substitute products that humans will accept is limited by our ability to act on our tastes, whereas animals are typically fed the cheapest balanced diet. The energy in animal diets, therefore, can be provided by products ranging from root crops to the citrus pulp produced as a waste product of orange juice processing. An important economic implication of this abundance of sources of carbohydrates is downward price pressure. Although grains are far too important as an energy source to be wholly replaced by other products, the diversity of alternative sources of supply needs to be borne in mind.

Proteins

Proteins are more complex foods. In addition to the carbon, hydrogen and oxygen that make up carbohydrates, they contain nitrogen and, in some cases, sulphur. Proteins consist essentially of chains of amino acids, and they are found in all living cells. They are particularly important for nutrition at times of rapid growth. The nutritional adequacy of proteins, therefore, depends not only on the crude amount of protein a food contains, but also on its composition; that is, the bundle of amino acids it contains. Plants are able to synthesize amino acids from simple nitrogenous compounds. Animals such as cattle and sheep have complex stomachs[5] and are able to synthesize amino acids, but even they require some protein and have particularly great protein needs when young. For humans and other simple stomached animals, proteins comprise only a small proportion of the total diet, but they are

4 It is not only humans who have taste preferences. Cattle, for example, are often induced to eat more by the addition of sweeteners, and there is a story in the sugar industry that cattle often prefer cane molasses to beet molasses as a feed because it is somewhat sweeter.

5 Complex-stomached animals are known as ruminants. It is in the rumen that the synthesis takes place. Humans, like animals such as pigs and chickens, are simple-stomached, or monogastric. Since they cannot synthesize essential foods, they must be fed all the nutrients they need.

essential. In developed countries, humans get most of the protein they eat from animal products; from meat, eggs and dairy products, but grains are important sources of protein in developing countries.

In the case of wheat, it is not only the amount of protein that is important, it is its nature. The two most important proteins in wheat are gliadin and glutenin, which together are known as gluten. Wheat is the only cereal that has glutenin in any quantity. This gluten has the property of elasticity when subjected to manipulation, and it is what gives a wheat-flour dough its rubbery texture and makes it well suited to bread production. The operation of yeast in a dough causes the release of gases, but the gluten traps these in small bubbles, preventing their escape. It is this which causes Western-style bread to rise, making it light, in sharp contrast to breads made from other cereals.[6] At the same time, this gluten makes finely-milled wheat rather unsuitable for direct feeding to animals; its elasticity makes it difficult to chew and digest. Of course, wheat is produced with a great variety of protein contents. In the US, for example, there are five major classes of wheat grown, whose protein content is summarized in Table 1.1.

Table 1.1 Protein ranges for US wheat classes

Wheat class	Protein range (%)
Hard Red Spring	12–18
Durum	10–16
Hard Red Winter	9–14
Soft Red Winter	8–12
White	8–11

What determines the protein content of wheat? In part, it is the variety, and in part it is climate. Generally speaking, hot, dry conditions lead to higher protein contents, but they also tend to lead to lower yields. Thus the highest protein wheats tend to be spring wheats grown in the Great Plains straddling the US/Canadian border, exposed to the hot, dry summers of the region. Lower protein wheats, grown in wetter climates, are suitable for animal feed, since they contain less gluten. This issue is dealt with in greater detail in Chapter 4.

There are two important economic aspects of the protein/carbohydrate balance in grains. Firstly, grains suitable for direct human consumption are more valuable than those suitable for animal consumption. Secondly, protein is more valuable than carbohydrate. Protein foods generally have good calorific value, whereas carbohydrates do not necessarily contain proteins.

6 Gluten also acts as a kind of preservative. Thus breads made from wheats with a high gluten content (i.e. a high protein content) tend to stay fresher for longer than breads made from low protein flours.

These two factors are closely related, but they are not simply different ways of saying the same thing. What makes high-protein wheat valuable is the fact that its gluten allows it to be used for the production of products for which humans have a pronounced taste. While it is true that the gluten and the protein content are the same thing, it is wheat's bread making quality, not its nutritional value, that is important in determining its price.

For both of these reasons, a positive correlation is found between a grain's protein content and its price. Of course, there are many nuances to this relationship, which will be explored later in the book, but it is useful to bear it in mind.

The uses of grain

Most grain that is destined for direct human consumption is processed. The simplest form of processing is grinding the grain into flour, and the most important use of wheat flour is, of course, bread. Higher protein wheats (which produce so-called strong flours) are used in most Western style breads, and lower protein wheats are used for arabic-style flat breads, where rising properties are less important.[7] Low-protein wheats are also used for biscuits and cakes. The Chinese make noodles from wheat flour, and Italian-style pastas are made from durum wheat, a hard, high-protein wheat whose flour is known as semolina. This type of wheat is also used for couscous. Large amounts of wheat are also fed to animals, especially in Europe and the USSR.

Millet is an important human food in much of Africa, and oats is found in uses as varied as animal feed (especially for horses) on the one hand and breakfast cereals on the other. Maize, in the form of tortillas and corn breads, is a staple in much of Latin America and is also well known in Europe and the USA as a human food, in the form of sweetcorn and popcorn. Its major use, however, is as an animal feed, having a high carbohydrate content and therefore a valuable energy source for growing animals. The range of foods made from grain is, of course, extremely wide, but bread is, in quantitative terms, by far the most important.

Grains fed to animals are not normally processed. Maize, for example, is normally fed directly. Of course, this is a slight simplification: with modern

7 French breads are made from low-protein flours. Hence the loaves are not as thick as with breads commonly baked in the US or UK; more gluten is needed to allow a thick loaf to rise. The low-protein content of French bread also explains its tendency to go stale very quickly.

combining, the ears of maize are shelled in the field, and the grain is normally dried to ensure it is in a proper condition for storage. It may also be mixed with other feeds. Wheat is usually crushed or rolled before being fed to pigs, cattle and sheep, but is fed whole to poultry. Grain farmers often retain on the farm part of their harvest for feeding. Specialized livestock farmers may buy whole grain or pre-mixed feeds that are nutritionally balanced for particular needs, but even in this latter case the processing involved is no more than mixing grain with other feedstuffs in certain proportions.

Grains are also used in a variety of processing industries that are somewhat more complex than flour milling. They are, for example all used in the production of alcohol. In Scotland, the best whisky is made from barley, but in North America whiskey is made from both maize and rye. Potatoes are said to make the best vodka, but grains are widely used. Distillers generally buy the cheapest and most convenient material to be their fermentable carbohydrate, unless they are making a premium brand of spirits. In many parts of Africa, millet is the basis of a thick, frothy beer.

Another important processing industry that uses grain is wet milling. High fructose corn syrup (HFCS), known as isoglucose in some countries, is a liquid sugar substitute found in soft drinks and in baked goods. It is a product of wet milling maize. Starch is also produced and, in its turn, is a feedstock for a wide variety of industries. Starch is used in human food (in confections, sauces and to make baking powder), in the brewing industry, to make adhesives and in a number of applications in industries as diverse as textiles, painting and ceramics.

Chapter 5 deals with these uses of grain in more detail. It should be borne in mind, however, that these processing uses of grain are, in quantitative terms, of minor importance. Grain has its importance because of its role in human food supply.

The origins of grain

Grain not surprisingly, has a long history. Indeed, the history of grain is as long as the history of agriculture and, therefore, of civilization. Our earliest human ancestors were hunter/gatherers, dependent for food on what they could find. As early as 7,000 BC, however, settled agriculture appeared in the valleys of the Tigris and Euphrates rivers in the Middle-East, and archaeologists have identified recognizable strains of wheat dating from this time. The discovery (if that is the right word) of cultivation practices coincided with the domestication of wild sheep and goats. It appears, therefore, that, from the earliest times, grain was being used as both human food and animal feed.

It is by no means certain, however, that animals were being kept for meat. Even in ancient Greece, where livestock husbandry was widespread, animals were kept primarily for milk, wool, skins and draught power. Although meat was eaten by the earliest cultivators, it seems more likely that there would be occasional slaughter of animals (on feast days, for example) than dedicated raising of animals for meat. But however much was being fed to animals, by 6,500 BC both wheat and barley were being cultivated quite widely throughout the area now encompassed by Turkey, Iran, Iraq and Israel.

Of course the earliest settlers were producing only for self-sufficiency. The emergence of towns, however, required the production of a surplus beyond the needs of farmers and their families, and this surplus seems to have emerged very quickly after the beginning of cultivation.

By 5,000 BC, maize was being cultivated in what is now Mexico. It is believed that a wild grass, 'teosinte', that is still found in Mexico, may be maize's ancestor. Maize was, of course, the basis of the Maya, Inca and Aztec civilizations, but when Columbus took the plant back to Europe its nutritional properties were not appreciated, and it was only grown as a curiosity for a long time. Around the same time, 5,000 BC, wheat and barley had spread into Africa, and by 4,000 BC grains had spread from the Middle-East into what is now Italy and Germany. Some 500 years later grain was being cultivated in more northerly regions of Europe; in what is now Northern France, Britain and Denmark. It was the increasing cultivation of grains that led to the widespread deforestation of Europe in the period 3,500 - 3,000 BC.

The new farming practices spread east from the Tigris and Euphrates, as well as west into Europe. In the Indian sub-continent, farmers were growing wheat as early as 4,000 BC. By 2,300 BC farmers in what is now Kashmir, Sind, Rajastan and the Punjab, on both sides of the border between India and Pakistan, were growing wheat, barley, peas, sesame, cotton and rice.

CHAPTER

2

A brief history of the grain trade

As discussed in Chapter 1, the history of grain is as old as the history of agriculture, and the emergence of civilization required farmers to produce a surplus beyond the needs of their local communities. In one sense, therefore, the growth of towns and cities required the growth of trade in grain, and the history of grain trade could be thought to be as long as the history of civilization.[1] However, if our understanding of trade is limited to exclude overland shipment for short distances and focused only on the kind of activity that is more generally thought of as international trade, then the history of trade in grain is considerably shorter than the history of its production. For much of human history, grain has not normally been shipped more than short distances, from a region's farms to its towns. The eminent French historian Braudel has estimated that as recently as the sixteenth century less than one percent of the total grain produced in the Mediterranean area was shipped internationally.[2] Of course, in response to particular circumstances great resources could be poured into trade: thus in

1 The beginnings of civilization are usually placed around 4,000 BC. Certainly, by 3,500 BC the Sumerian civilization was flourishing. This was at least 3,000 years later than the development of agriculture.

2 See Braudel, *Civilization and capitalism 15th–18th centuries: Volume 2, The Wheels of Commerce*, p402.

response to a severe crop failure in Tuscany at the end of the sixteenth century, the Venetian, Tuscan and Genovese leaders arranged for massive shipments of grain to relieve famine. Such events were not usual, however, and throughout the period from the end of the Roman Empire to the modern age, international trade was concentrated in low-bulk, high-value products such as spices, silk and ivory. Even when international trade in wool and fabrics started to grow at the start of the modern era, shipment of bulky products like grain was very limited. One major reason for this was cost: transport, especially overland, was extremely expensive, and these costs could only be borne by high-value products destined for consumption by the rich.

International shipment of grain, however, is not an invention of the modern age. In Ancient Greece and Rome for example many important features of the modern trade were already in operation.

Ancient Greece

Ancient Athens was perhaps the first major civilization to be dependent on grain imported from distant lands. Much of the land around Athens was (and is) unsuitable for grain cultivation: olives and livestock, however, could do well. Solon, a key leader of Athens while its power was developing, encouraged specialization in these crops and the development of industry (especially pottery), thereby increasing the dependence on imported grain. By the time of Demosthenes it was recognized that the Athenians were more dependent on imported grain than any other of the city states.

About one-half of the needed grain was imported from the Crimea. The trade was in private hands, with merchants generally buying grain on credit (advanced by private banks), chartering independent vessels and usually travelling with the cargo to ensure its safe arrival. But the Athenian authorities were reluctant to entrust the city's food supply entirely to private merchants. The protection of the major sea routes, and in particular the route through the Dardanelles, was a prime issue of public policy. In 426 BC Athens decreed that a fine of 10,000 drachmae would be levied on any guardian of the Hellespont who stopped or interfered with any shipment of grain through the straits. There were also a number of attempts to establish direct control of the sea routes via the establishment of colonies. Settlers were installed on the Aegean islands of Lemnos and Imbos in 499 BC; Byzantium was put under siege and captured in 478 BC, and Skyros, in the Aegean, was colonized in 476 BC. As one historian of the period has written:

> . . . summarily, large tracts of Athenian history in the fifth and fourth centuries (and indeed down till the Roman

> period) can be written round her absolute need to control, or prevent other powers controlling, the sea-route from the Crimea through the Hellespont across the Aegean to Piraeus which brought her the corn without which her population would starve. Either she controlled the Dardanelles, or she had to be subservient to the power which did.[3]

Ironically, it was the development of the naval power needed to defend these shipping routes that posed a threat to Athens' neighbours, and led to the destabilization of the balance of power within the network of Greek city states. The logistical problems of feeding Athens paled next to those that faced Ancient Rome, a city that may have had a population close to a million at its peak. Supplying grain to the capital of the Roman Empire required a formidable network of international trade, whose political and economic aspects are fascinating.

Ancient Rome

Rome's food supply problem began to become acute when Italian grain production started to decline in the second century BC. This was taking place at the same time as Roman power, and the population of Rome, was growing. The provision of grain to feed the city was one of the major preoccupations of public policy. Grain shortages were common, and famines were not unknown. Key officials in Republican Rome, the aediles, were charged with the duty of providing Rome with the grain to keep the people fed and the circuses that were the primary form of popular entertainment: hence the origin of the phrase, 'bread and circuses'. In the early years, they discharged this duty in a rather erratic and ad hoc fashion, relying on moral pressure on merchants to bring extra supplies to Rome at times of shortage. When serious shortages threatened, the aediles could advance credit to merchants to buy grain, and they could release to the market the grain which had been taken in taxation. Overall, however, in this early period there was no established system of public intervention in the private market that brought grain to Rome. Partly in response to this disarray, and partly because the problems of food supply were becoming more serious, a populist leader, Gracchus, established in 123 BC a law which brought the

3 See Davies, *Democracy and Classical Greece*, p59. 'Corn' is used here in the British sense, meaning 'grain', not 'maize'.

public authorities directly into the grain market, and had implications for grain supply until the end of the Empire.

The Gracchan law required the state to have grain on sale at a price equal to or lower than the normal price. Any citizen could buy this grain, although the quantity each citizen could buy was limited. This explicit introduction of intervention by the state, and its possible implications for the finances of the government, caused considerable opposition, and the Gracchan Law was soon abolished. The principle having been established, however, was not to go away. Other laws governing grain supply were passed, and in 58 BC free distribution of a fixed quantity of grain to each citizen of Rome was enacted. When Caesar took power, he cut the number of recipients of this free grain from the 320,000 to which it had risen, to 150,000, and fixed it at this number in perpetuity. This system did in fact last for four centuries, with the entitlement to free grain eventually becoming a kind of honour, bestowed by the state on deserving citizens or sometimes sold to a rich person who craved the 'honour'.

The Roman Empire, apart from taking over this system of limited free distribution of grain, took an active role in the general provisioning of its capital city. It did this in a number of ways and it did it for two reasons. Firstly, the state was uniquely well suited to take a role in trade: it had an unrivalled network of information sources, in the form of its magistrates throughout the Empire. It also imposed taxation in the form of grain, and therefore had the storage facilities needed in locations around the Empire. Secondly, the political importance that was attached to the grain supply and consequently to the seat of the Empire made the state willing to intervene in the market, sometimes selling grain at a loss at times of scarcity, in order to preserve stability. Of course only the state had pockets deep enough to be able to intervene so comprehensively.

Organization of the grain trade

How was the grain trade organized, and what kind of role did the state play in the everyday activity of shipping grain to Rome? In the first place, it appears that direct price controls were rare. There certainly were examples of intervention in pricing: Tiberius subsidized prices one year, and one of the most complete examples of economic information that has survived from Ancient Rome is Diocletian's edict on maximum prices, published in AD 301. This edict fixed maximum prices for products as diverse as grain, beer, olive oil and meat and also established wage levels in occupations such as carpentry, farm-labouring, teaching and advocacy.[4] Such regulations remained in force for very little time and the state had to rely on other techniques to keep grain supplies adequate and prices at levels that would not provoke social disorder.

Rome was fortunate in being close to the sea and therefore able to be supplied by ships from grain producing areas around the Mediterranean. Egypt was Rome's principal supplier, accounting for about one third of the city's total needs. The balance of the grain came from other regions within the Mediterranean basin. The quantities involved are not certain, but one source refers to shipments from Egypt to Rome of 20,000,000 modii (140,000 tons approx) per year during the reign of the Emperor Augustus. The Roman port of Ostia handled these imports, and its facilities were improved in AD 42 specifically to allow better handling of grain. Excavations in the port have revealed the offices of over 60 different agencies involved in shipping and commerce. These same excavations have shown a number of practices similar to those in use today: warehouse space was rented out and grain was used as collateral for loans.

The fleet that brought grain to Rome was privately owned, and shipowners tended to be independents who carried cargoes either on their own account or on consignment. There was an elaborate system of quality control on the grain trade. When vessels were loaded, samples were taken and placed in pottery jars that were then sealed and placed in the custody of the guards who travelled with the shipments. When the cargo reached its destination the quality of the shipment was compared with that of the sample. The ships used on the main trade route, from Alexandria to Rome, were 1,200 - 1,300 tons and posted an average speed of about three knots. A speed of five knots, or 100 miles per day, was exceptional, but by no means unknown. (This compares to a typical speed of a grain vessel in the modern world of around ten knots.)

The Emperor Claudius, who was himself jostled by a mob protesting about food shortages in AD 51, took particular care to ensure merchants had adequate incentives to supply Rome with her grain. He guaranteed to cover any merchant's losses of grain caused by storms while the grain was in transit. He also gave a series of special privileges to shipowners and

4 This edict provides fascinating insights into relative prices in the ancient world. Wheat was fixed at 100 denarii per army modius (a unit of measure approximately equal to a quarter of a bushel); the price difference between whole and ground grain was 100%; chickens were set at 30 denarii each; oysters were 1 denarius each; a barber was allowed to charge 2 denarii per client and a carpenter was to be paid 50 denarii per day, although he was also to be provided with his maintenance. Uncertainty over exactly what the units of weight are limits the amount of useful analysis that can be done with these data. They do seem to confirm, however, what should not be a surprise, that grain was very much more expensive, in real terms, than it is today.

shipbuilders. Most notably, a non-Roman who built a ship and used it to bring grain to Rome for six years would be granted Roman citizenship, an honour not conferred lightly. Generally, merchants who handled the city's grain supply were exempt from all forms of public service: it was deemed that their work securing grain was a sufficiently onerous duty.

Remarkable though it may seem to make this claim, it is the case that the sophistication of the grain trading system used to provision Rome was not equalled until the nineteenth century. From the time of the collapse of the Roman Empire until the growth of world agricultural trade in the eighteenth century, trade was heavily concentrated in items for the rich. There simply was no economic way to transport bulky products over large distances, and particularly overland.

Britain

The advent of the modern era brought many changes in world trade, but it was not until the repeal of Britain's Corn Laws in 1846 that there came into being an import market large and important enough to make an impact on trade flows as dramatic as that of Ancient Rome.

London had been an important market for grain for many centuries: as early as 1534 Henry VIII prohibited grain exports to ensure adequate supplies for the capital, and under Elizabeth I the Privy Council received monthly reports on the city's grain supply. Advances in agricultural technology, however, alleviated the shortages these measures implied, and in the century from 1660 to 1760 Britain was a net grain exporter.

The growing demand for grain associated with the rapid growth in population in the eighteenth century, however, outpaced domestic production. By 1795 Britain was importing large quantities of grain from Europe. The difficulties with imports during the Napoleonic Wars, and the political pressure that the landowning interest was able to bring to bear, led to the regulation of imports, and in 1815 wheat imports were prohibited when the domestic price was equal to or less than 80s a quarter.[5] There was, however, a growing conflict between the landowners, on the one hand, and the expanding

5 A quarter is an imperial measure of grain. It is equal to 8 bushels. A bushel was originally a measure of volume, whose weight equivalent varied from one grain to the next. These weight equivalents have now been established, however, and a bushel of wheat weighs 60 lbs. A bushel of maize weighs 56 lbs. Until the standardization of these measures, the weight of a given volume of grain could vary because of variation in its moisture content, so one must use these early figures with caution.

class of manufacturers; the Industrial Revolution was creating pressure for cheap grain imports, so that wages could be kept low. The manufacturing interest triumphed in 1846, when the Corn Laws were repealed and the British market was opened for wholesale importation of grain.

It is hard to overstate the implications of this for the history of agriculture and trade in the nineteenth century. Cheap grain allowed wages to be kept down and in turn fueled Britain's economic growth. At the same time, British capital was exported all around the globe to secure the supplies of grain that the country needed. Table 2.1 sets out the simple facts of the growth of the British grain import market in the nineteenth century.

As the table shows, the repeal of the Corn Laws allowed a dramatic increase in British grain imports, and although the initial surge was in grains other than wheat, wheat remained by far the most important grain. If one adds together imports of wheat and flour, then it is apparent that food grain needs accounted for well over half of imports throughout this period. It is, however, the growth and sheer size of the market that impress the most, with imports of almost ten million tonnes by the outbreak of the First World War. A closer look at the data shows that in the 1860s imports began to grow at a particularly dramatic rate.

To understand this, it is important to look at who was supplying Britain with its grain in the nineteenth century, information that, for the case of wheat, is provided in Table 2.2. In the following discussion, it should be borne in mind that it was in this period that a recognizable modern grain trade emerged; most of the market practices and institutions that are an

Table 2.1 UK grain imports, 1840–1914 (five year annual averages; thousand tonnes)

	Wheat	**Flour**	**Other grain**	**Total**
1840–44	401	56	116	574
1845–49	503	157	645	1,306
1850–54	833	218	620	1,671
1855–59	813	157	747	1,717
1860–64	1,463	284	879	2,626
1865–69	1,514	213	1,407	3,134
1870–74	2,012	259	2,057	4,328
1875–79	2,642	386	1,600	4,628
1880–84	2,926	676	2,824	6,426
1885–89	2,850	813	3,185	6,848
1890–94	3,327	955	3,561	7,844
1895–99	3,520	1,041	4,536	9,098
1900–04	4,120	1,006	4,572	9,698
1905–09	4,846	645	3,993	9,484
1910–14	5,309	533	4,018	9,860

Source: Calculated from data in Mitchell, *Abstract of British historical statistics.*

Table 2.2 Sources of UK wheat imports, 1829–1914 (five year annual averages; thousand tonnes)

	Russia	Prussia	Germany	Canada	USA	Argentina	India	Australia
1828–32	51	71	0	15	3	0	0	0
1833–37	2	25	0	5	0	0	0	0
1838–42	46	163	0	5	5	0	0	0
1843–47	56	112	0	10	25	0	0	0
1848–52	142	137	0	5	41	0	0	0
1853–57	132	152	0	15	147	0	0	0
1858–62	229	0	290	76	371	0	0	0
1863–67	411	0	325	46	229	0	0	0
1868–72	640	0	229	112	544	0	0	0
1873–77	457	0	188	168	1,087	0	127	71
1878–82	340	0	152	173	1,753	0	224	137
1883–87	406	0	91	127	1,300	15	518	152
1888–92	823	0	86	107	1,087	112	528	112
1893–97	833	0	41	168	1,524	391	234	102
1898–02	229	0	36	335	1,920	472	305	193
1903–04	1,107	0	0	396	640	996	1,107	356
1905–09	772	0	0	645	919	1,179	726	432
1910–14	696	0	0	1,072	1,138	711	945	640

Note: Prussian shipments are included in the total for Germany from 1858.

Source: Calculated from data in Mitchell, *Abstract of British historical statistics.*

important part of today's grain trade first appeared in the nineteenth century, and they were developed by traders supplying the unprecedented British import demand.

At the time of the repeal of the Corn Laws, Britain was relying for most of its imports on Europe. There were two principal trade routes: the first, from Odessa in the Black Sea, through the Dardanelles, across the Mediterranean, through the Straits of Gibraltar and up to Britain, is reminiscent of the dependence of Ancient Athens on grain from the same region. The second was from the Baltic ports and across the North Sea. Indeed, the wheat price in Danzig was the key market price, reflecting the importance of the port and the grain from the East European plain that was shipped through it. London was the most important grain port in Britain at this time.

During the 1860s, however, two developments had an important influence on the trade. In the first place, growing demand in Britain's industrial heartland in the North of England allowed the northern ports, and particularly Liverpool, to grow at the expense of London. The greatest boost to the Liverpool trade, however, came from the other significant development, the emergence of the USA as a large scale supplier.

Liverpool had always been the British port to which Californian wheat had been sent, but its rapid growth came when the end of the US civil war and the opening up of the Great Plains, thanks to the rapidly expanding railroad network, allowed US grain production to grow. In 1868, Liverpool added new facilities to its port, allowing it to accommodate grain ships as large as 5,000 tons. It was the largest grain port in Europe.

At the same time, improvements in international transportation (particularly the introduction of steam-powered ships, replacing sailing vessels[6]) allowed the product of the prairies to be shipped to Britain at ever-falling costs. In the period 1868–1979, for example, it cost 11s a quarter[7] to ship wheat from Chicago to Liverpool; by 1886, it had fallen to 6s 2¼d. In 1892 the cost was 4s 3d and in 1902 it was below 3s. In other words, the cost of transportation dropped by two-thirds over the thirty years from 1870 to 1900. Another important factor was the sharp devaluation of the US dollar that took place at the end of the Civil War.

As Table 2.2 makes plain, it was not only the United States whose productive land was planted to put bread on British tables. In the 1870s Australia began to export wheat to Britain; in 1873 the opening of the Suez Canal allowed Indian wheat to be profitably shipped to Britain, and these two were joined in the 1880s by Argentina. To a certain extent, these supplies were replacing European suppliers, particularly Germany, whose domestic needs were growing as a result of industrialization, but there was also considerable competition among suppliers. In the mid- and late 1880s, British imports from the United States fell, causing considerable consternation in the mid-west.[8] This competition, which resulted most importantly from the expansion of production in the low-cost areas of Argentina and Australia, was a key cause of the agricultural recession of the 1880s.

This dramatic internationalization of the grain market was inevitably associated with major changes in the organization of the trade. Reflecting the emergence of the US as the leading exporter, Chicago became the pre-eminent grain market in the world; the grain market had been established there in 1848, and by 1865 futures contracts in grain were being traded there. In 1866 a telegraph cable was laid across the Atlantic, allowing a close link between the Chicago and the Liverpool markets, and in 1883 futures trading began in Liverpool. (Liverpool merchants wanted their own market, partly because it could deal in CIF prices, and partly because they distrusted the

6 It appears that steam power was most competitive on the transatlantic run. Sailing vessels were still being used to ship California's wheat around Cape Horn to Liverpool: and in 1891 a four-masted sailing vessel carried a cargo of 5,200 tons of wheat to Britain, setting a record for the largest sail-powered cargo. But California's wheat producers were not able to compete with producers elsewhere and production was shrinking even before this record was set.

7 Recall that a quarter is 8 bushels.

8 In the 1880s the complaint was heard that the US was losing market share to Indian suppliers, a competition often deemed unfair because, it was believed, the rupee's exchange rate against sterling gave an advantage to Indian supplies. This kind of concern has resurfaced more recently.

Chicago market, which they thought was prone to speculative excesses.) The cable also had a profound effect on the trade: the more rapid transmission of information reduced the importance of stock holding in the UK, and increased the importance of brokers.

At the same time the spread of the trade across national borders facilitated the emergence of the large grain trading companies that are still important players in the market a century later. The five biggest companies, Cargill, Continental Grain, Louis Dreyfus, Andre and Bunge, (see Chapter 9), all came to prominence in the turbulent grain trade of the second half of the nineteenth century.

By the outbreak of the First World War, the world's grain trade was recognizably modern, in that it had developed almost all of the features that it exhibits today. One could plausibly argue that the period just before 1914 was the apogee of the free-market grain trade: government intervention in the free movement of grain around the world was probably less at that period than ever before or since. Of course grain was every bit as important as it had ever been, and governments kept a watch on the trade. But the day to day business of growing, shipping, marketing and processing grain was remarkably free of the heavy hand of governments.

The story of the grain trade from the outbreak of the Great War in 1914 is, in large part, the story of a growing involvement of governments. To understand the economics of the modern grain market, this brief history must be brought up to date, see Chapter 3.

CHAPTER

3

Grain in the global political economy

Raw materials remain critically important to the world's political economy. Although more and more economic activity (to say nothing of popular interest) is centred on services and the high-value added high technology industries, the plain fact is that trade flows in raw materials still command the attention of policy-makers. Of course, agricultural commodities do not enjoy the spotlight as much as oil, for example, but food security remains an important political issue in the Soviet Union,[1] China and much of the developing world. Agricultural trade has also been a serious irritant in relations between countries within the OECD, (witness the long-standing dispute between Japan and the US over rice).

Agricultural goods, and particularly basic commodities like grains, have a special claim over governments. As foodstuffs they meet essential human needs, and as agricultural products their production is subject to the vagaries of the weather. They also have an economic and political importance by virtue of accounting for a large amount of labour. Given these factors, it is perhaps not surprising that governments have frequently sought a degree of involvement in agricultural production and trade. Grains have not escaped this governmental embrace; the two decades or so prior to the First World

1 See author's note at the beginning of this book.

War were unusual in the looseness of this embrace, and it was quickly tightened as soon as the war erupted.

Wartime controls on prices and trade were slowly lifted after the war's end, and the recovery from the war led to a brief period of prosperity for farmers. By 1921, world production had recovered and prices for most major crops began to fall. For the rest of the 1920s, prices were very unstable, reflecting both changes in world production levels and macroeconomic instability; economic difficulties in the UK and Germany, for example, affected their demand for grain. For much of the decade, therefore, competition among exporters was intense.

The 1930s

In the early 1930s agriculture suffered greatly; the Great Depression and the beggar-thy-neighbour trade policies that were widely adopted caused trade volumes to shrink (the value of world trade dropped by 20% during the crisis, and trade in foodstuffs dropped by 25%) and also had the effect of pushing prices sharply downwards. Wheat prices halved between 1927 and 1931, for example, and there were similar price falls for other foodstuffs. This led to considerable dislocation in farming areas around the world, and prompted a response by governments.

The initial response by governments to the crisis in agriculture (as it was to the crisis in industry) was to raise tariffs. Tariff levels on foodstuffs more than doubled in most European countries between 1927 and 1931, for example. Even Britain, whose rejection of agricultural protection in the nineteenth century was so important an influence on the growth in world trade, succumbed to protectionism; fruits and vegetables were made subject to duty in November 1931 and by the end of 1932 wheat had also been brought under the tariff. In fact the British tariffs had little real impact, since the exports of the Empire entered duty-free, but they were of considerable symbolic importance.

These trade measures, however, were insufficient to keep domestic prices at levels satisfactory to producers in Europe, and obviously only made the situation worse for exporters.[2] Hence governments began to intervene more extensively in the markets. France, in 1936, saw the creation of the Office National Interprofessionelle du Ble, charged with fixing the wheat price and regulating exports and imports. In the US, the Agricultural

2 Producers in North America suffered more than most. Not only did export prices fall, but volumes shipped also collapsed. Grain exports by the US and Canada more than halved between the mid-1920s and the mid-1930s.

Adjustment Act of 1933, one of the landmark laws of the New Deal, created federal authority for massive intervention in agriculture; payments were made to farmers for reducing their acreage and the Commodity Credit Corporation came into being to extend guaranteed prices to farmers by giving them loans against the security of their crops.[3]

In addition to these national responses, there was an attempt to co-ordinate intervention in the wheat market at the international level, with the signing, in April 1933, of the International Wheat Agreement (IWA).[4] This was not the first example of such co-ordination, (the Brussels Sugar Convention of 1902 had enjoined exporters from subsidizing exports), but it was a remarkable attempt to address at an international level the problems of grain trade in the 1930s.

Under this agreement, which was to run for two years, exporters agreed to limit their exports and to reduce their production by 15% in the second year. Importers agreed not to increase wheat production, to reduce tariffs if world price rose and to take measures to increase consumption. It will come as no surprise to those who followed international commodity agreements in the 1970s and 1980s to learn that the 1933 IWA was a failure. Exporters did not take the necessary measures to reduce production and Argentina exceeded her export quota. Neither quotas nor the acreage reduction plan could be agreed for the second year, and the Agreement was allowed simply to expire in 1935. As with the economy as a whole, it took the Second World War to push grain prices back up; the War also brought more extensive controls over agriculture and economic activity generally.

The 1950s

The experience of the 1930s was, of course, very important for economic policy generally, and the apparent lesson of that time, that government

3 The price support works because the crops are valued not at the market price, but at a governmentally decreed price. If market prices stay low, the farmer forfeits his crop and keeps the 'loan', if prices rise, he reclaims his crop, sells it at the higher price, repays the loan and pockets (most of) the difference.

4 This was only the first of many International Wheat Agreements. Every so often the idea of international co-ordination of the wheat market appeals to one government or another, and debate starts on the desirability and practicality of using international agreements to stabilize commodity prices. Examples of successful agreements are few and far between; examples of failed agreements are legion. The literature examining them is also extensive. There is currently an International Wheat Agreement, but it has no price-stabilizing role, and confines itself to acting as an information clearing house.

intervention in markets could at least mitigate the cycles of capitalist economies, certainly had an impact on agriculture. The policy instruments created in the US and elsewhere remained in place and, perhaps more importantly, the political coalitions whose interests these policies served remained too powerful to be crossed. But the war had another significant influence on the world grain trade. The emergence of the US as the undisputed leader of the West and its clear dominance of the global economy produced the unprecedented situation that the leading economic and political power was a grain exporter. From Ancient Athens through medieval cities to Victorian Britain, economic power was concentrated in grain importers, and imperial policy, to the extent that it focused on grain, was concerned with securing supplies at low prices from overseas. From the 1950s on, however, US policy was more concerned with maintaining prices and securing access to markets.

Price maintenance became, effectively, the responsibility of the US government, since the policy mechanisms of the 1930s remained in place. Of course, prices were routinely set at levels higher than those needed to meet market demand for grain: the inevitable result was the accumulation of surpluses, whose financial cost was borne by the government.

The problem of surpluses was less than it might have been, thanks to rapid advances in the meat industry. Rising consumer incomes in the post-war period led to a sharp increase in the demand for meat, and the widespread adoption of techniques of intensive animal raising led to an expansion in demand for feedgrains; some land was diverted from wheat to maize and to soybeans to meet this demand. Nonetheless, government owned stocks continued to rise and world prices remained pretty much at the US support level throughout the 1950s and 1960s. Clearly, in the longer term, the US position, as the largest producer and one unwilling to let its producers take their lumps on the world market, is untenable. High support prices result in burdensome stocks and in incentives for producers in other countries to expand production; market-clearing prices are probably at too low a level to be acceptable to the political representatives of the grain farmers.

One important aspect of the search for markets for US grain has been food aid. Large scale food exports were provided under the 1948 Marshall Plan, and in 1951 a loan of $190 million was provided to India to pay for imports of US foodgrains. The 1953 Mutual Security Act provided for sales of surplus commodities to friendly governments for local currency. In 1954 the Agricultural Trade Development and Assistance Act, better known to the world as Public Law 480 or PL 480 was passed. This act, pragmatically meeting the desire to provide humanitarian assistance and helping with the problem of disposal of surplus commodities, provided for donations, barter sales and local currency sales of grain.[5] There were some years during the 1950s when aid shipments of grain under PL 480 exceeded commercial exports.

An additional purpose of the Act was to develop future commercial markets for grain, and this has happened to a certain extent: Brazil, South Korea and Sri Lanka, for example, received large concessional sales in the 1950s and 1960s and emerged as major commercial wheat importers.[6]

Over the longer term, surplus disposal through mechanisms like these proved inadequate, and the US began, in the mid-1960s, to make supply control more attractive to farmers, and as a result stock levels began to drop. This set the stage for some dramatic changes in the global grain market in the 1970s. Before turning to these developments, however, it is worth mentioning another important feature of the 1960s: the emergence of the European Community's Common Agricultural Policy (CAP).

An outline of the key operational features of the CAP is presented in Chapter 4, but it was apparent even when the policy was being formulated in the early 1960s that it was going to have a significant impact on world markets. The policy came into force in 1967 and was designed to protect European farmers from import competition by establishing high and stable prices for their products. At the time, the US opposition to the policy was muted, for three main reasons. In the first place, US political interests were advanced by the strengthening of the European Community (a clear case of sharp conflict between the USA's interests as a superpower and as a grain exporter). Secondly, there was some failure to perceive just how protectionist the CAP was; and thirdly, the US was optimistic about the possibility that US access to the EC market could be secured through general liberalization under the General Agreement on Tariffs and Trade (GATT). Indeed, during the Kennedy Round of GATT negotiations, under pressure from the Americans who were trying to bring agriculture under the mantle of the GATT, the EC proposed what became known as the 'montant de soutien', under which all forms of support to agricultural producers would be frozen at the then-current levels; but the US rejected this offer, on the grounds that it would entrench protectionism and constituted a retreat from the goal of full liberalization. In retrospect, and particularly in the context of the difficulties

5 In 1969 the decision was taken to replace local currency sales with sales on long term, soft credit. Although these changes did reduce the aid component of the sales by requiring some hard currency expenditure on the part of the importer, PL 480 remains essentially a food aid programme.

6 The large volume of shipments under PL 480 prompted a debate about whether these shipments were genuinely helpful to the recipient countries. While no-one disputes the value of famine relief, many people have argued that the availability of subsidized imported grain has a disincentive effect on local farmers, and contributed to dietary shifts among consumers that tend to increase the dependence of poor countries on food imports. It has been argued that countries have invested heavily in port facilities to cope with imported grain when they should have invested in building up their domestic agricultural capabilities.

posed by agricultural trade issues in the GATT Uruguay Round, nearly thirty years later, it is easy to see that the EC's offer should have been grabbed with both hands, but the opportunity was lost.

The 1970s

The 1970s brought a number of major changes in the world's grain economy. Perhaps the most significant was a policy change in the Soviet Union, made after rioting in the Polish cities of Szczecin and Gdansk in 1970. These riots occurred immediately after increases in food prices but were also a protest against general economic conditions, including the lack of good food (especially meat) and poor housing. Fearing similar unrest in the USSR, the Soviet leadership allocated more funds for housing and agriculture, but also decided that future crop failures could not be absorbed by the Soviet consumer and that the longer term development of adequate meat supplies would require grain imports. Accordingly they began to import grain in earnest, beginning with the 'Great Grain Robbery'.[7] The Soviet Union had been a grain exporter until the late 1950s; in the 1960s, it made some imports and some exports, but was not a major player in the grain trade. The policy shift of the early seventies presaged the emergence of a huge new import market for both wheat and coarse grains. Although Soviet import levels have varied considerably from year to year and a number of policy initiatives have been taken by the Soviet authorities to reduce import dependence, the USSR has become the largest grain import market in the world.

This significant policy switch in the USSR came at the same time as a number of other developments, all of which were closely inter-related. The early 1970s saw the macroeconomic disturbance of the breakdown of the Bretton Woods system of fixed exchange rates, which led to a fall in the

7 This term refers to the Russian grain purchases in the early 1970s, when representatives of each of the main grain trading companies were summoned to Moscow and each, in turn, was given substantial orders. Each firm was unable to believe its luck, and naturally did not share the information with its competitors. As a result, prices in the US market did not begin to respond until a large part of the purchases had been made. This was no more than clever buying on the part of the Soviet Union, but when the full scale of the purchases became known, there was an outcry in the US, where people felt the Russians had effectively bought up the government stockpile of grain at bargain basement prices. The increase in Soviet imports certainly was remarkable: in the crop year 1970/1 their imports totalled 0.3mn tonnes; in 1971/2, 3.4mn and in 1972/3, 15.0mn. The USDA instituted an export sales reporting system after this episode to ensure a better flow of information to the markets.

value of the dollar. This increased the competitiveness of US grain on world markets, but was also a symptom of macroeconomic disequilibria that were to cause a variety of problems in the early 1970s. To compound these problems, in 1973 the Arab oil boycott of the OECD led to a sharp rise in oil prices, increasing the inflationary pressure on the Western economies. In addition a series of small disruptions within agriculture caused agricultural commodity prices to move up sharply, and the 'World Food Crisis' of 1972–3 was born.

Having lived through the 1980s, it is hard to take seriously the tone of debates about agriculture that took place in the early 1970s. Although (many, though by no means all of) the poor countries of the Third World[8] were adversely affected by the commodity price boom of the early 1970s, the problem of poverty did not worsen significantly, and the World Food Conference in Rome in 1974 would not have been convened had the plight of the Third World not provided a suitable vehicle for other, more powerful interests. The atmosphere of the early 1970s was very much one of fear of scarcity, exemplified by the difficulties in the oil market. There was also a widespread feeling that the US and its allies could use 'food power' as a countervailing force against OPEC's 'oil power'.

For a variety of reasons, some to do with the grain market itself, others more connected to macroeconomic disturbances, grain prices rose very sharply in the early 1970s. Although prices quickly fell after the 1973 spike, they remained above the levels of the 1960s. These higher prices (and heavy investment in agricultural land as a hedge against the inflation that was emerging as a serious problem) led to increases in grain production, and to increases in the support prices paid to grain farmers in most producing countries. They were heady days of expansion, particularly in the US where farmers, borrowing money at negative real interest rates to acquire an asset, land, whose value seemed to keep on rising, pulled land out of government set-aside programmes and set about producing grain to meet the new demands from the Soviet Union and the oil-rich OPEC nations. During the 1970s, agricultural exports accounted for about 20% of total US exports.

The 1980s brought an end to the party mood of the mid- and late 1970s. This time, the key influences on the grain economy were macroeconomic. Monetary policy changes in the US, enacted in October 1979 as part of an attack on inflation, produced a sharp upward movement in interest rates. This brought an end to the period of cheap borrowing and had a number of significant effects. On the one hand, borrowers as varied as farmers in Iowa and developing country governments were suddenly faced with massively increased debt service costs: costs they could not meet and that

8 Many less developed countries benefited from higher prices for their commodity exports, a benefit that more than offset the loss from higher food import bills.

precipitated both the Third World debt crisis and a similar farm belt debt crisis in the US. Under the twin effects of this interest rate shock and the second oil shock following the deposition of the Shah of Iran in 1979, the world's economy fell into a severe recession. At the same time, the newly-elected President Reagan embarked on a fiscal policy that created enormous federal deficits; the need to finance these at a time when US savings were low and falling meant that interest rates stayed high to attract a flow of foreign funds into US government debt securities. This created upward pressure on the international value of the dollar. Since grain prices are denominated in dollars, and since US agricultural policy had been framed in the 1970s, setting unrealistic price levels, producers in other countries found local currency prices attractive enough to expand production profitably while their US counterparts were going bankrupt in numbers that reminded many observers of the 1930s.

The detailed features of the grain market over the past ten years or so are presented in subsequent chapters.

Soviet-American relations

One of the most intriguing aspects of the global grain trade is the relationship between the USSR and the USA. From the perspective of the early 1990s it is easy to forget the intensity of 'Great Power' conflict in the recent past, but since the Soviet decision to rely on grain imports, grain has played a significant role in Soviet-American relations. From the Soviet side, the dependence on imports is regarded as highly undesirable, and there has also been a determined attempt to minimize dependence on a single supplier. Nonetheless, reliance on the US has, for practical purposes been unavoidable.

On the American side, there has always been a conflict between the desire to serve the interests of the agricultural community and the crusade against communism. When the Soviets first opened up to significant volumes of trade, Kissinger was running foreign policy from the Nixon White House, and he sought to use grain trade as a diplomatic weapon. Prior to 1970, Soviet-American trade was running at about $200 million a year; in 1970 and 1971, Soviet traders brought half a billion dollars worth of grain from the US. Kissinger saw the opening grain trade as the chance to open up another channel of contact, another type of engagement between the two superpowers that could help pave the way for better relations. The administration's favourable policy towards the grain sales was also helpful in political terms: 1972, after all, was an election year. Under President Ford, a long term agreement between the two countries was concluded to regularize the trade a little and to provide a symbol of the growing closeness of superpower relations.

Under President Carter, concerns over the farm sector were less pressing, and the President experimented with the 'food power' rhetoric of the 1970s. Following the Soviet invasion of Afghanistan, an embargo on grain sales in excess of the minima in the long term agreement was imposed. It is now widely recognized to have been a failure. Both the EC and Argentina increased their shipments, and the impact on the Soviet Union, far from a withdrawal from Afghanistan was a determination to minimize dependence on American supplies. The loss of US market share in the USSR was, therefore, a more lasting effect than any change in Soviet foreign policy.[9] Moreover, the experience of this failure had the effect of encouraging the US to seek multilateral approaches to grain trade, providing support for the American determination to see agriculture treated in the GATT Uruguay Round.

President Reagan revoked the embargo shortly after coming to office, and during his administration the contradiction between rhetoric and reality reached new heights. While building up US defence expenditure and committing substantial resources to the 'struggle against communism', Reagan's administration subsidized grain sales to the Soviet Union to an unprecedented extent and replaced the 1975 long term agreement with a new one that provided for greater levels of trade between the two countries.

The radical reforms in the Soviet Union introduced by President Gorbachev and the economic difficulties that have followed have not lessened the country's need for grain imports. Nonetheless, their ability to pay for these imports certainly has been impaired and these new political realities have made it much easier for the US administration to support Moscow's purchases.

Developing countries

There is often an association made between developing countries, grain and food aid. For all the tremendous importance of international responses to famines, it is important to keep in mind that this kind of food aid is not quantitatively significant in relation to the commercial grain market. In a typical year in the 1980s, the total volume of grain classified as food aid

9 For a good discussion of the embargo, see Paarlberg, *Lessons of the grain embargo*. Of course, the Soviets did eventually withdraw from Afghanistan, but no-one has claimed that this was in any way connected with the grain embargo.

amounted to just under ten million tonnes, which represents about 5% of world trade. Moreover, a large part of what is counted as food aid (according to the Food Aid Convention, a part of the International Wheat Agreement) is not exactly famine relief: preferential shipments of grain by the US to its favoured allies, such as Egypt, are counted as food aid, for example. Also, one must face up to the fact that surplus disposal has always been a prime motivation behind food aid.[10]

Food aid aside, developing countries play a central role in the grain economy. Argentina is one of the major grain exporters, but it is as commercial importers that developing countries are most important. Although many developing countries are major producers of grain, they have, generally speaking, not been able to generate significant exports. Some people have argued that the growth in developing country imports of grain is a bad thing. Imported grain, cheaper than it should be because of the excess production by protected farmers in rich countries, enters a poor country, depresses the prices faced by local farmers, encourages consumers to switch to Western diets rather than diets based on locally produced foodstuffs and distracts governments from the task of building up their own agricultural systems. Others point out that the growing popularity of Western diets is an inevitable consequence of economic growth, and that governments are right to buy food from the cheapest source rather than getting trapped into the pursuit of self-sufficiency; a goal that could only be achieved at a very high budgetary and economic cost, at least in most developing countries.

Whatever the merits of either side, the fact remains that developing countries are now very important as commercial importers of grain; details are presented in Chapters 5 and 6. The growth in developing country imports is a recent phenomenon and can be traced to the rapid economic growth that was enjoyed in much of the developing world in the 1960s and early 1970s. The countries that have emerged as significant importers are,

10 Those interested in the debates surrounding food aid, and particularly the issue of whether it would not be simpler to write a cheque instead, should read Hans Singer et al, *Food aid, the challenge and the opportunity*. There are indeed many interesting questions about food aid, and particularly about the political roots of the disasters that create a need for aid. There used to be famines in India, the response to which was food aid. But good policies enacted by the Indian government have had a major, beneficial effect on the country's food situation, and a serious drought in 1987 was experienced without the kind of distress that would have been experienced in the past (or elsewhere). India turned to the world market for a small level of imports and did not experience a crisis. Moreover, a number of governments, especially in sub-Saharan Africa, have become dependent on food aid as one of the few forms of resource transfer that does not have policy conditionality. Food aid is indeed a complex issue, from the moral, political and economic points of view.

for the most part, either those that have considerable oil wealth or those that have been able to generate reasonably rapid economic growth.

The USA and the European Community

During the 1980s, agricultural trade moved to a position of prominence in global policy making circles. The renewed attempt to bring agricultural trade under the discipline of the GATT, in the Uruguay Round of negotiations, is the most obvious sign of this prominence. The persistent difficulty in reaching agreement on this matter when progress was possible on other thorny issues, such as textiles, trade in services and intellectual property rights, indicates just how intractable agricultural issues have become. Although the Uruguay Round deals with agriculture, the fact is that grain lies at the heart of the debate; and the key debate is between the EC and the US. There are, of course, other players, notably the Cairns Group, a grouping of smaller agricultural exporters in which Australia has played a leadership role, and Japan, whose market for a number of goods remains closed or tightly restricted, but agreement between the Americans and Europeans would not run into serious obstacles put down by other parties.

At the heart of the dispute between the US and the EC is the level of commitment to free trade. The US is much more committed to it than is the Community. Within the EC, the liberal voices of the UK and the Dutch are overruled by the interventionist French, and although the Germans have adopted a liberal stance on other issues, on agricultural matters they side with the French.[11] When it comes to agriculture, the Community's position has traditionally been that it wishes to preserve the viability of rural communities, and it is prepared to impose huge costs on its own consumers, taxpayers and the rest of the world to achieve this. The US position has always been that markets should be free to allow comparative advantage to work.

The dispute took on new intensity in the 1980s, however, because the protectionist policies of the EC led to the emergence of an export surplus of grain: hence the US began to feel competition in third world markets as well as losing sales in Europe. The US view is that this strikes at the heart of

11 At the root of this behaviour is an electoral calculus. Post-war German governments have needed the support of farmers, especially in key regions where the Free Democrats are very powerful. Indeed, for virtually the entire period of the mounting crisis in agriculture, the Germans had the same agricultural minister, the formidable Herr Keichle, who has never demonstrated an interest in the costs of protecting European farmers.

its interests as an agricultural exporter; hence securing a reduction in EC subsidies became a *sine qua non* of the negotiations. The EC, for its part, has continued to offer only modest reductions in subsidy programmes. Moreover, the changed climate in superpower relations cannot be overlooked as a factor: US dislike of the CAP has been moderated in the past by support for Europe as a bulwark against the Soviet Union. With such a bulwark no longer needed, the US is likely to become a much tougher negotiator on a range of issues involving the Community.

The CAP has always been very costly in economic terms, but its budgetary cost has also, at times, been so great that measures have had to be taken to limit it. The rapidly rising budgetary cost is creating a climate within the EC favourable to reform, and it may be that these reforms will cut back subsidies sufficiently to form the basis of a GATT agreement. Yet the EC does not have a good record on trade and agricultural matters, and it can be confidently predicted that the European attitude to agriculture will continue to cause tensions in relations with countries more disposed to free trade.

PART

II

Production, consumption, trade and prices

CHAPTER

4

Grain production

Grain and its climatic requirements

Grain is grown very widely throughout the world. The range of climatic conditions under which grains can flourish is quite remarkable and contrasts sharply with the demanding requirements of many other crops. This reflects in part the diversity of crops covered by the term 'grains', even excluding rice. One grain crop, maize, can be grown in an astonishing variety of conditions: from 58 degrees north to 40 degrees south; from below sea level to altitudes as high as 12,000 feet; in sub-tropical areas of Florida and in the semi-arid plains of the Soviet Union; in parts of North Africa where average annual rainfall is less than ten inches and in areas of the Indian sub-continent where rainfall exceeds 200 inches. This is not to say that there are not areas where maize will not grow: in fact, it is, in its own way, a demanding plant, requiring both sunshine and certain amounts of moisture at particular times to ensure its growth. Its light requirements are an important reason why it is not grown widely in northern Europe.

Conditions that are adverse for one grain can often favour another. Oats, for example, need moisture and cool temperatures to flourish. Cool nights, especially when the plant is mature, are important. Oats can also grow on soils that are too acidic for wheat or barley, and rye is hardy enough to survive on poor, light, acidic soils where other grains would fail.

Perhaps the single most tolerant grain, however, is wheat. Wheat is, after all, the most widely produced grain, and there is scarcely a month of the year in which wheat is not being harvested somewhere in the world. It is also remarkably tolerant of dry conditions. The climate in which wheat is grown has a critical influence on protein levels: hot, dry summers produce high levels of protein and, as a result, the highest protein wheats (known as hard wheats) come from the North American prairie, on both sides of the border between the USA and Canada. Conversely, the cooler, wetter climate of Europe produces a lower protein, or soft wheat.

Another important distinction is between winter and spring grains. Maize is always planted in the spring and harvested in the autumn, and this is the traditional pattern for all grains. Both barley and, more importantly, wheat, however, are grown as both winter and spring grains. Take winter wheat in the northern hemisphere as an example. It is planted in September or October, and then grows to a height of five to seven inches before the onset of winter. This stand of wheat can be grazed by cattle, a marked advantage for many farmers. Over the winter, the plant becomes dormant, ideally being covered by snow. The snow covering protects the dormant crop from damage caused by cold weather: 'winterkill' can be a serious problem if there is severe weather and no adequate snow cover. As soon as spring arrives, the plant resumes growth, and it is normally ready to harvest by July. Spring wheat, on the other hand, is planted as early as possible in the spring, matures over the summer and is ready for harvest in September.

Each type of grain has its own advantages. Spring wheat generally has a higher protein content, since winter wheats typically do not have enough exposure to the dry heat of summer to develop a high-protein content. (Some winter wheats are as high in protein as some spring wheats: on average, however, their protein content is lower and the highest protein wheats are spring wheats.) Moreover, spring wheats can be grown in areas where the winter weather is too severe to allow crops to survive (in large parts of Canada and the USSR, for example). On the other hand, winter wheats tend to produce higher yields than spring wheats.

The climatic requirements of grain production, therefore, do not limit it to only a few areas of the world. Of course, production is concentrated in a small number of areas, but grains are grown widely. The requirements for successful cultivation vary from one region to another and the climate imposes constraints on the particular grains that are available for any individual farmer to produce. It remains true, however, that grains can be successfully cultivated on a very large proportion of the world's arable land.

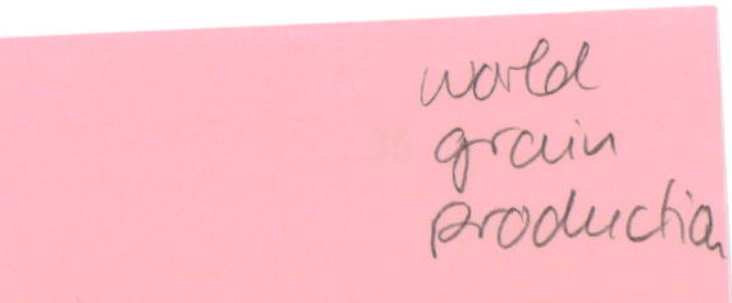

Production patterns – a long term view

Figure 4.1 plots a long term series of grain production data and has a number of important features. The growth in production is striking: in less than 30 years, world grain output has increased from under 1 billion tonnes to 1.8 billion. On the other hand, this growth has hardly been even. On several occasions, production has fallen below that of previous years, and the falls were particularly pronounced in 1983 and 1988. Note, however, that production of wheat has been much less volatile than production of grains as a whole. Indeed, world rice production (which comprises the difference between total grains on the one hand and wheat and coarse grains on the other) has also grown steadily. This suggests that much of the volatility is caused by coarse grains.

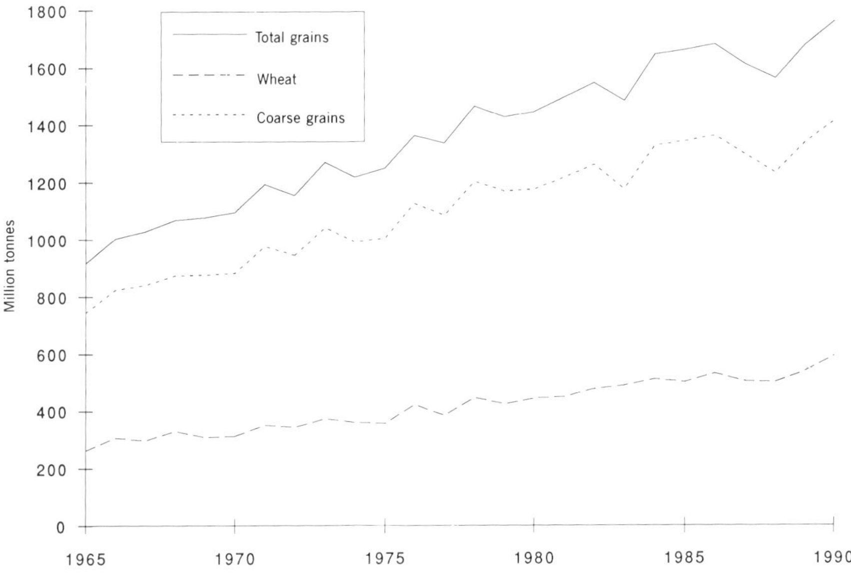

4.1 World grain production.

Table 4.1 shows the growth of world production over the past 30 years. As the data indicate, grain production has grown at an annual average rate of almost 3% over this period. This is, by historical standards, a rapid growth rate. Over the entire period 1885–1939, world production of wheat grew at an average annual rate of only 1.3%.[1] There are, unfortunately, no comparable data on world coarse grain production for this earlier period, but the comparison of the wheat production growth rates for the two periods is instructive.

There is one other interesting comparison to be made between the two

1 Computed from data in Malenbaum, *The world wheat economy 1885–1939.*

Table 4.1 Growth rates of world grain production, 1961–88

	1961–88	1970–88
Wheat		
Developed countries	2.9	3.2
USSR	0.7	−1.0
Developing countries	4.9	4.7
World	3.1	2.8
Coarse grains		
Developed countries	2.4	1.6
Developing countries	2.6	2.2
World	2.6	1.8

Note: Growth rates are least squares trend growth rates.

Source: Computed from data of the Economic Research Service (ERS), US Department of Agriculture (USDA).

periods. In the 1920s and 1930s, it was widely held that world average yields were constant. Although there were variations from region to region and from year to year, because of fluctuations in the weather and differences in the productivity of soil, yields certainly were very stable. The growth in output, therefore, had to come from increases in the area cultivated. In the more recent period, however, most of the increase in production has come through increases in yield. According to one study[2] of the growth in grain production over the period 1960–1983, 74% of that growth came from increases in yields. In fact, to the extent that there was a growth in area cultivated, it occurred in the 1960s and early 1970s. Since the late 1970s, the area of grain harvested has fluctuated around a stable level.

One other interesting feature of the data is the lack of uniformity in the growth in production. Output in developing countries has grown more rapidly than in developed countries. Growth has been particularly rapid in Asia: annual average growth rates of wheat production for the period 1961–88 were 6.0% in Asia as a whole, 6.4% for India and 6.8% for China.

The rapid growth in production in the past 30 years has been associated with an increase in the instability of production. The most complete analysis of this changing pattern[3] concluded there were a number of reasons for this, but they were all related to a fundamental feature of the grain economy; the extensive spread of high-yielding seed and cultivation technologies. This has had the important consequence that farmers in different regions are exposed to similar problems: they face similar fertilizer prices, and similar risks from crop disease.

2 Hazell, P B R, *Sources of increased variability . . .*

3 *Ibid.*

The overall pattern, then, is that world grain production has grown steadily and quite quickly in the recent past, but that this production growth has increasingly become dependent on increments in yields rather than areas, and that production instability has become more pronounced.

Production of wheat

Table 4.2 presents data on wheat production over the 1980s. The countries selected are the world's largest producers, plus Canada, Australia and Argentina, whose production is not large but who are significant exporters, and whose production therefore is of importance to the world market. World production was 442 million tonnes in crop year 1980/81, exceeded 500 million tonnes for the first time in 1984/5 and reached 537 million tonnes in 1989/90. The Soviet Union was the largest wheat producer for many years, but its position has, in recent years, been under threat from China, whose production virtually doubled in the 1980s, from 55 million tonnes in 1980/81 to 91 million in 1989/90. Production in India and the European Community also grew steadily in this period.

It is also apparent from the data that not all producers have participated equally in the growth of production. Production in the USA has been erratic, but clearly has not shown an upward trend. In the Soviet Union, production has not grown, and in some countries, notably Australia, production has been extremely unstable. In 1982/3, Australia produced only 8.7 million tonnes, but the following year output was 22 million. In percentage terms, this is the most remarkable production swing of the entire decade, but many other producers have faced similar problems.

Over the past 30 years, it is yields that have become the key variable in

Table 4.2 World wheat production (million tonnes, July/June years)

	80/1	**81/2**	**82/3**	**83/4**	**84/5**	**85/6**	**86/7**	**87/8**	**88/9**	**89/90**
USA	64.6	76.2	76.4	65.9	70.6	66.0	56.9	57.4	49.3	55.4
Canada	19.2	24.8	27.6	26.5	21.2	24.3	31.4	26.0	16.0	24.3
Australia	10.9	16.3	8.7	22.0	18.7	16.2	16.2	12.4	14.1	14.1
Argentina	7.8	8.1	14.5	12.8	13.2	8.5	8.9	8.8	8.4	10.2
EC-12	61.5	58.1	64.7	63.8	83.1	71.6	72.0	71.4	74.7	78.5
USSR	98.2	80.0	84.3	77.5	68.6	78.1	92.3	83.3	84.4	92.3
China	55.2	59.6	68.4	81.4	87.8	85.8	90.0	85.8	85.4	90.8
India	31.8	36.3	37.8	42.8	45.5	44.1	47.1	44.3	46.2	54.0
Others	64.3	62.3	66.3	61.4	61.3	68.1	76.7	73.9	77.9	73.3
World	441.5	448.6	479.3	489.5	511.8	499.8	530.7	503.1	501.2	537.1

Source: Economic Research Service, USDA.

determining production. Table 4.3 shows yield data for the same producers as Table 4.2 and provides more insights into what is behind this pattern of production variability. Note the three distinctive features of these data. Firstly, there is the steady increase in world yields, from 1.87 tonnes per hectare in 1980/1 to 2.38 in 1989/90. Most individual producers also show an increase, and it is particularly marked in China, India and the EC. Yet there is a great deal of variability in yields, and this variability has two aspects. On the one hand, there is a pronounced difference between yields in different countries: yields in the EC in 1980/1, for example, were higher than any other producer achieved by crop year 1989/90. EC yields are now approaching 5 tonnes per hectare, and there is a club of farmers in the UK, the ten-tonne club, who have achieved yields of ten tonnes per hectare. Only in China are yields even beginning to approach EC levels. On the other hand, there is variation within one country from one year to the next, i.e. the variation in Australian production as discussed. Table 4.3 shows the importance of yields in explaining this. Argentina, Canada and the USSR have also experienced great yield volatility in the 1980s.

There are two, interrelated reasons for this. Clearly, the weather is very important, and one cannot explain Australian yields, for example, without reference to droughts. Canada and the USSR are both exposed to extreme climates that can produce good crops one year and bad crops the next. The second reason, however, is agricultural policy. It certainly is not favourable weather that has made the EC such a productive wheat grower, nor can weather explain the growth in yields in China and India. Agricultural policy will be discussed later in this chapter when production of coarse grains has been reviewed.

The United States, as these tables make plain, is not the world's largest producer, nor has its production been growing impressively in the recent past. Yet the country is perhaps the most important producer and the largest exporter of wheat. Since the major wheat futures markets are in the

Table 4.3 Wheat yields in selected producers (tonnes per hectare)

	80/1	**81/2**	**82/3**	**83/4**	**84/5**	**85/6**	**86/7**	**87/8**	**88/9**	**89/90**
USA	2.25	2.32	2.39	2.65	2.61	2.52	2.32	2.53	2.29	2.20
Canada	1.74	2.00	2.13	1.93	1.61	1.77	2.20	1.93	1.23	1.79
Australia	0.96	1.38	0.77	1.70	1.55	1.38	1.45	1.36	1.57	1.58
Argentina	1.55	1.40	2.05	1.85	2.22	1.61	1.79	1.84	1.79	1.86
EC-12	3.94	3.71	4.04	3.97	5.13	4.68	4.58	4.50	4.82	4.83
USSR	1.60	1.37	1.47	1.53	1.34	1.55	1.89	1.78	1.76	1.94
China	1.89	2.11	2.45	2.80	2.97	2.94	3.04	2.98	2.97	3.04
India	1.44	1.63	1.69	1.82	1.84	1.87	2.05	1.92	2.00	2.24
World	1.87	1.88	2.01	2.14	2.21	2.18	2.33	2.28	2.29	2.38

Source: Economic Research Service, USDA.

US, and because of the link between prices in the US and those in the world market (a link that will be explained in Chapter 7), any analyst of the grain markets needs to pay particular attention to developments in the US. Table 4.4 shows some more detailed production data from the US. Production is broken down by major classes of wheat: the importance of this breakdown will become obvious later. Hard wheats are the higher protein wheats used in baking breads, and hard spring generally has a higher protein content than hard winter. Durum wheat is used to produce Italian-style pastas and, in North Africa, to make couscous. Soft winter and white wheats are used to make cakes and biscuit flours, although the Chinese use white wheat to make noodles and are the main importers of white wheat.

These data are reported in bushels, not tonnes. While a simple conversion factor can be used,[4] it is unfortunately the case that both units are commonly in use in the trade. The US futures markets, for example, quote prices per bushel, whereas trade data (and production data outside the US) are usually quoted in tonnes, so anyone studying the market needs to be able to work in both units.

There is one feature of this table that deserves close attention. In the summer

Table 4.4 US wheat production by class (million bushels)

	1985/6	1986/7	1987/8	1988/9	1989/90
Hard Spring	460	451	431	181	433
Durum	113	98	93	46	92
Hard Winter	1,230	1,018	1,021	882	711
Soft Red Winter	368	292	348	473	548
White	254	232	216	232	251
Total	2,425	2,092	2,107	1,812	2,036

Source: Economic Research Service, USDA.

of 1988, the US experienced a long and severe drought, and a fall in grain production was an inevitable result. Note, however, that there was not a uniform impact on wheat production. The sharpest fall occurred in spring wheat production (it is spring wheats that are the most exposed to the weather over the summer). Yet it was also the case that hard winter wheat was affected more than soft winter; this reflects the geography of the drought's impact, which was greater in those regions where hard winter wheat is produced. White wheat, production of which is concentrated in

4 A bushel of wheat weights 60 lbs; hence one bushel is 0.027216 of a metric ton. Alternatively, there are 36.74 bushels in a metric ton. Note the conversion factor for maize is not the same, since a bushel of maize weighs 56 lbs. Hence its conversion factor is 0.0254.

the Pacific north west of the country, was hardly affected at all by the unusual weather.

Production of coarse grains

The coarse grain market is a little more complex than the wheat market, reflecting two factors. Firstly, there are a number of different grains included, although one could argue that this is no more complex than the different classes of wheat. Secondly, a large proportion of coarse grain production does not leave the farm on which it is grown, being fed to the animals raised there. There is also a substantial amount of wheat, grown as animal feed, that does not leave the farm, but off-farm processing is needed to turn wheat into flour and flour into bread. The most important implication of this is that the market for coarse grains is rather different than that for wheat. Some aspects of this will become obvious below.

Table 4.5 shows a breakdown of world coarse grain production by the three major grains. Maize is by far the most important grain, both in world production and trade, accounting for over half of world output. Barley is a distant second and sorghum, and the other grains, have production levels that are very much lower. Although the other grains are traded, the greatest interest is concentrated on maize. There is a futures contract in Chicago on maize.

Table 4.6 breaks down world production by major producer. As in the case of the discussion of wheat above, the selected countries are either major producers, or major exporters (or both). Some similar patterns are clear, particularly the variability of production from one year to the next. US production fell from 217 million tonnes in 1987/8 to 150 million the following year, thanks to the drought in the summer of 1988. Production in Argentina fell by almost 50% in the same crop year, and South Africa's crop was practically halved in two successive seasons between 1980/1 and 1982/3. There has

Table 4.5 World coarse grain production by the three major grains (million tonnes, October/September years)

	80/1	**81/2**	**82/3**	**83/4**	**84/5**	**85/6**	**86/7**	**87/8**	**88/9**	**89/90**
Maize	406.0	437.3	443.9	347.5	458.7	479.8	474.3	448.8	400.5	460.8
Barley	163.2	156.2	165.3	164.8	174.8	177.2	182.4	181.2	167.9	169.5
Sorghum	58.7	68.7	66.7	59.2	66.1	70.5	64.5	56.4	55.4	55.6
Total (incl other)	731.7	766.4	783.9	687.2	814.0	841.7	831.8	793.9	731.2	800.3

Source: Economic Research Service, USDA.

Table 4.6 Coarse grain production by major producer (million tonnes, October/September years)

	80/1	81/2	82/3	83/4	84/5	85/6	86/7	87/8	88/9	89/90
USA	198.3	246.6	250.7	137.1	237.6	274.8	252.1	217.0	149.7	221.5
USSR	80.5	69.4	91.8	101.9	90.5	100.0	105.9	113.7	97.5	104.8
China	82.4	79.5	81.8	91.6	96.2	82.3	87.0	95.8	94.2	94.6
EC-12	82.6	76.1	80.7	73.9	90.4	88.9	81.7	82.4	88.1	82.0
Canada	21.8	26.0	26.6	20.9	21.6	23.9	25.5	25.5	19.7	23.5
Argentina	21.0	18.4	16.6	17.4	19.3	17.4	13.0	13.1	7.3	8.1
South Africa	15.3	8.8	4.8	5.1	9.0	8.9	7.9	7.9	13.0	10.0
Thailand	3.5	4.5	3.7	4.3	4.7	5.7	4.6	2.9	4.4	4.2
World	731.7	766.4	783.9	687.2	814.0	841.7	831.8	793.9	731.2	800.3

Source: Economic Research Service, USDA.

also been pronounced variation in the output of the Soviet Union. Another interesting similarity is the importance of many of the same countries in both wheat and coarse grains. The US, the EC, China and the Soviet Union are the key producers of both wheat and coarse grains, accounting for well over half of world production.

There are, however, two important differences. In the first place, the dominance of the US is marked. No single wheat producer has regularly accounted for more than 20% of the world wheat crop, but the share of world coarse grain production held by the US has normally been between 25 and 30%, only falling below this level in abnormal circumstances. Further evidence for this is provided by the selection of countries for the table: Argentina, South Africa and Thailand are important exporters, see Chapter 6, but their production levels are small in relation to world production. A corollary of this dominance is the importance of maize, since maize is by far the most important coarse grain grown in the US.

Secondly, production in China has grown only modestly, and production in the EC has not grown at all, a marked contrast to the position in wheat. Some further insights into this are provided by Table 4.7, where data on yields of coarse grains are provided.

Table 4.7 Coarse grain yields in selected producers (tonnes per hectare)

	80/1	81/2	82/3	83/4	84/5	85/6	86/7	87/8	88/9	89/90
USA	4.80	5.68	5.80	4.17	5.45	6.04	6.07	6.12	4.56	5.97
USSR	1.39	1.19	1.58	1.66	1.53	1.71	1.81	1.91	1.69	1.87
China	2.60	2.59	2.74	3.04	3.30	3.05	3.12	3.33	3.33	3.32
EC-12	3.87	3.64	3.91	3.72	4.51	4.38	4.13	4.34	4.60	4.42
Argentina	2.57	3.80	3.03	3.03	3.14	3.56	3.70	3.19	3.46	2.94

Note: Argentine yields refer to maize only.

Source: Economic Research Service, USDA.

As is the case with wheat, there are some sharp differences between producers. US yields are approaching 6 tonnes per hectare, whereas Soviet yields are only approaching 2 tonnes per hectare. Yields in both the EC and China have been going up, but nowhere near as quickly as their yields of wheat. Their yields have also been going up more swiftly than their production, indicating that land has been leaving the production of coarse grains: in fact, it has been switching into wheat.

The dominance of the US in world coarse grain production, the fact that maize dominates US production and the very high yields achieved there together have an important implication for world production. The so-called corn belt, a swathe of land in the central US from Ohio to Nebraska, is where US maize production is concentrated. Soil and climatic conditions in this region are very favourable for maize (and, indeed, for soybeans); but these conditions tend to be very similar across the entire region. This means that adverse weather conditions in this one region can have a significant impact on global production. This is not the case for wheat. Consider the drought of 1988, which hit the mid-western states of the US very hard. As a result, US coarse grain production fell from 217 to 150 million tonnes whereas in the rest of the world, production increased from 577 to 581 million tonnes. Therefore, world production fell from 794 to 731 million tonnes, a fall of 8% in global production simply because of adverse weather in one region of the United States. The same drought had no significant effect on world wheat production.

The point is vividly illustrated by Figure 4.1, in which the longer term trend in grain production is plotted. The sharp dip in coarse grain production, and in total grain production, is plain. The same graph indicates that such disruptions to world production are not that unusual. Indeed, just five years earlier, in 1983, world output fell sharply and, as can be seen, it was coarse grain output that accounted for the fall. A glance back at Table 4.6 shows that US production in 1983/4 was more than 100 million tonnes lower than the previous year. Although the weather was adverse in the mid-western states that year, the fall in production was unusual in that it owed a great deal to a deliberate attempt by the US authorities to reduce production.

Policies and their impact on production

It would obviously be possible to write an entire book simply on agricultural policies in the major producers and the impact of these policies on the grain market. The analysis of agricultural policies is taken very seriously by economists, especially in the United States, where their views are taken rather more seriously than in most other producing countries.

Agricultural policy is not as old as agriculture, but it is known from the Bible that storing grain in years of plenty to make up for shortages in years of crop failure was an activity of the state in the earliest times. There are two important sets of reasons for the existence of agricultural policies, when, in most countries, there are not policies for, say, the plastics industry. The first set is economic, and has to do with the peculiar conditions of agricultural supply and demand. Completely free markets in agricultural produce would be very unstable, because demand is inelastic and supply is inherently variable because of the weather. This instability would greatly complicate decision making by farmers and consumers, and would not produce an economically efficient outcome.[5] The second set of reasons is political. Food is clearly very important, and countries attach great value to security of supply (although the fact that secure supply can be provided by international trade as well as by domestic production is often overlooked in political debates). It is also the case that farmers are often able to exert considerable political power, both through the electoral system and through the romantic ideas of farmers held by urban voters.[6] As a consequence, farmers in many countries are able to obtain massive subsidies from taxpayers and consumers in their own countries and, through expanding their production, to prevent more efficient farmers elsewhere from realizing the benefits of their greater efficiency.

Obviously, the economic arguments about the inefficiency of free market solutions and the political arguments about influence vary from commodity to commodity. One does not need to be unduly cynical about the political process to believe that economists' arguments about the desirability of public intervention when unregulated markets lead to inefficiencies carry little weight when politicians are deciding what kinds of agricultural policies to implement. They calculate the costs and benefits of policy options in a fairly straightforward way.

UK consumers may place great value on a secure supply of tea and coffee, and both markets are prone to great instability, but even the National Farmers' Union and the Ministry of Agriculture have not proposed a British policy

5 This argument is spelled out in greater length in almost every economics textbook. An interesting statement of the issue is contained in J M Boussard, *A French perspective on supply control and management*.

6 An electoral bias in favour of farmers can come about through failure to adjust constituency boundaries to reflect population movements: hence French rural constituencies tend to be smaller than urban and suburban ones, giving farmers more voting power. Alternatively it can be constitutional, as in the US, where each state has two senators, irrespective of its population. This gives disproportionate representation to low population farming states. Of course, the situation can be such that farmers are penalized: this often happens in developing countries, where the political pressure from urban consumers, who want cheap food, are stronger than the voices of a badly organized and badly educated farm sector.

that greenhouses be erected across southern England to grow these tropical crops. Since the budgetary costs of this would be formidable, consumers remain free to buy these products from efficient farmers elsewhere at competitive prices.

When it comes to grain, however, the position is somewhat different. It is produced in countries where farmers have a great deal of political influence. One should therefore expect that grain policy often has more to do with political factors than with ensuring economically efficient outcomes.[7] Nowhere is this more clear than in the debate over the importance of farm incomes. There is widespread concern in policy making circles that farm incomes not be allowed to lag too far behind incomes in the rest of the economy. This concern is frequently given as a justification for setting farm prices. Yet prices are not the same as income and economists have known for a very long time that raising prices for farmers simply results in farmers competing for land, driving up land values. Price supports, therefore, get capitalized into land values, benefiting landowners. To the extent that farmers are tenants, not owners, they do not benefit. Not surprisingly, however, it is landowners, not farmers (or at least it is landowning farmers) who have the greatest influence on farm policy.

In some small exporting countries, notably Canada and Australia, policies are typically geared at smoothing the fluctuations in farmers' incomes caused by variable outputs and prices. The opportunities to subsidize production are limited by the size of their economies. In Argentina, a major grain exporter, agriculture (particularly export agriculture) has typically been taxed rather than subsidized, a reflection of the limited political power of rural interests. In India and China, the political imperative to increase production to meet consumption needs has been important in creating a policy framework favouring the adoption of high-yielding seed varieties. In China, this has been a fairly recent phenomenon and only took place with the economic liberalization that followed the death of Mao Zedong and that allowed peasant farmers greater control over their production.

In order to understand the recent evolution of grain production, however, the policy framework in two of the most important producers and exporters, the US and the European Community needs to be discussed. These two are important, partly because of their size (the US is the leading exporter of both wheat and coarse grains) and partly because of their influence

7 There is one interesting study of the impact of agricultural policy in a number of countries. Roland Herrmann *Agricultural price protection, import dependence and economic development* analyzed data from 38 countries and found that the level of protection afforded wheat producers was a rising function of GDP per capita and a decreasing function of the degree of self-sufficiency. This suggests countries subsidize their farmers if they can afford to, but their willingness to foot the bill diminishes once domestic consumption needs have been met.

on the market. But it is also useful to bear in mind the broader international significance of the agricultural trade disputes between the US and Europe, described in Chapter 3. This conflict has its roots in agricultural policy in the two countries.

Agricultural policy in the European Community

The European Community's Common Agricultural Policy (CAP) has its roots in the European experience of food shortages during and in the years following the Second World War. The Treaty of Rome, which established the European Community, explicitly states that the Community is to seek security of supply for its food, although it does not mention that this is to be done through indigenous production. Europe has long been a large food importer, even though many European countries are major agricultural exporters. The existence of a large import requirement, the political power of farmers and the desire by policy makers to retain economic activity in the countryside to limit population movement to the cities were all important in determining the shape of the CAP, which went into force in 1967.[8] In broad terms, the CAP establishes domestic preference; it raises prices to domestic producers, restricts imports, and, by raising consumer prices, forces consumers to help pay for the policy. Taxpayers[9] also contribute, since there are large budgetary costs of the policy. Grains, and in particular wheat, lie at the heart of the CAP. The details of the policy, set out below, are instructive.

Each year, the Council of Ministers of the EC agrees an 'intervention price' for Ormes, in France, the location deemed to be that with the greatest grain surplus. This price, adjusted for transport costs, is the price at which the Community will purchase surplus grain from farmers. Simultaneously, a 'target price' is set for Duisburg in Germany, the location with the greatest

8 It was also long thought that there was a compromise between France and Germany on this: Germany wanted access to French markets for manufactured goods and to secure this had to give ground on agricultural policy. In recent years, however, it has become clear that Germany is an enthusiastic supporter of the CAP, because of its large number of small, inefficient farmers in the politically important Southern regions.

9 It is very important to realize that taxpayers and consumers are not one and the same. The difference is particularly important when one speaks of food products, the cost of which looms large in the budgets of poor people, many of whom may not be taxpayers. There are important issues of fairness in agricultural policy that are all too often ignored by those who trumpet concern about poor farmers but appear not to care about poor consumers, who are far more numerous.

deficit. Finally, a 'threshold price' is set for Rotterdam, and variable levies are assessed on imports such that, no matter what the world market price, grain does not enter the Community below the threshold price. The grain that the Community buys from farmers (at the intervention price) is exported; since EC prices are higher than those on the world market, this requires subsidies. Chapter 7 discusses in greater detail the relationship between prices in the EC and those in the world market.

There are a number of important features of this policy. In the first place, the policy has the effect of stabilizing prices between the intervention and the target prices. While this stability should make farmer decision making easier, one difficulty is the fact that price decisions are taken by the Council of Ministers, a political body. Because of the sensitivity of price setting, and the conflicting interests of different members of the Community, the Council often finds itself embroiled in long and difficult last minute negotiations, and prices are often not agreed until after farmers have completed their planting. Nonetheless, European farmers are certainly not exposed to great price volatility, and the level at which prices have been stabilized has clearly been an important reason for the dramatic growth in European wheat production as seen in Tables 4.2 and 4.3. European farmers have been able to expand their yields of wheat to such high levels because of the guaranteed prices they receive. Recall, however, that EC production of coarse grains has not increased, a reflection of the bias in prices in favour of wheat: Tables 4.6 and 4.7 showed that EC coarse grain production was unchanged over the 1980s, and that yields were lower than in the US. This is in pronounced contrast to the situation with wheat.

Secondly, there are three types of costs of the policy. Consumers pay higher-than-world-market prices for grain. In the case of bread, this results in substantial costs for individual consumers. In the case of those who buy grain to feed to animals, it pushes up their costs (and therefore the prices of dairy products, meat and eggs to final consumers) and has also created a frantic search for cheaper substitutes discussed in Chapter 5. A second type of cost is the budgetary cost borne by taxpayers. The Commission buys grain, stores it and subsidizes its export. Finally, there is a cost to other producers. The growth in EC production and exports of wheat has not only deprived other exporters of the once valuable EC market, but has also introduced a new competitor to the world market. How substantial are these costs?

The first and third costs are hard to measure, but there have been a number of studies that attempt to throw light on these important questions. With respect to an assessment of the impact on the Community's economy, two recent reports have reviewed the relevant studies,[10] and show results that

10 See International Monetary Fund, *The CAP of the EC*, and A Walters, *The economic consequences of agricultural support*.

vary considerably. At one extreme, one study of the CAP in 1976 found a deadweight loss equal to 0.13% of the Community's GDP.[11] At the other extreme, a more comprehensive study found a deadweight loss of 2.7% of the Community's GDP in 1985. Of course, these are the net costs to the economy as a whole. There are massive transfers from consumers and taxpayers to producers: the most recent study[12] of these estimated that, in 1985, the cost to consumers was US $49.0 billion, the cost to taxpayers was US $2.2 billion and the gain to producers was US $27.2 billion. These sums are enormous: a deadweight loss to the economy of 2% of GDP should not be belittled.

The impact on producers outside the EC has been twofold. Since the EC's exports of wheat have risen faster than world trade, other producers have lost market share. Perhaps more importantly, however, the EC has depressed world prices. A large number of studies[13] of this price effect have concluded that EC policies have reduced world wheat prices by between 8% and 17%. One study of the impact of EC and Japanese policies concluded that, together, these two countries depress world prices by up to 50%.[14]

These costs for overseas producers were substantial enough for them to make farm trade reform a central concern of the GATT Uruguay Round, as seen in Chapter 3. Clearly, other producers would not have risked this had it not been for the direct threat to their interests posed by the EC's emergence as an exporter.

All these studies share the conclusion that the cost to taxpayers, that is the budgetary cost of the policy, is dwarfed by the transfers from consumers to producers and the impact on producers elsewhere. Yet the budgetary cost is the only cost that is directly, unambiguously and accurately measurable, and it is the cost most directly felt by policy makers. The costs of subsidizing grain exports reached a gross level of 3.157 billion ECU in 1987, up from only 92 million ECU in 1974. Of course, this rise in costs had been to some extent foreseen; and because the budgetary burden was becoming insupportable in the late 1980s, a number of measures were introduced to reduce the

11 Note this is just the deadweight loss. This study also found a loss to consumers of 3.9 billion ECU, a loss to taxpayers of 0.2 billion ECU and again to farmers of 4.7 billion ECU.

12 Rod Tyers and Kim Anderson are two academic economists in Australia who have done a great deal to expose the follies in agricultural policies around the world. Interested readers will find several of their works cited in the bibliography, and the figures quoted here are presented in all of the cited studies.

13 See Koester, *Policy options for the grain economy . . .*, Schiff, *Information, expectations and policies*, Sarris & Freebairn, *Endogenous price policies . . .*, Mielke & de Gorter, *Impacts of the common agricultural policy . . .* and Paarlberg & Sharples, *Japanese and European Community agricultural trade policies*.

14 See Carter & Schmitz, *Import tariffs and price formation . . .*

costs. Moreover, there was some sensitivity in the Community to the risk to relations with the United States posed by ever expanding wheat exports. In fact, there were those who had been warning about rising costs for many years, but in the early 1980s, the high value of the US dollar, in which currency wheat prices are denominated, meant that the ECU costs of export subsidies were smaller than they would otherwise have been. Hence it was not until the dollar began to decline against the European currencies that the budgetary burden began to grow. The response to this rising cost was two-fold. On the one hand, the Commission took a number of formal measures. The intervention price was not increased at all in 1986, 1987 and 1988, and was cut by 3% in 1989. In 1986 a system of 'co-responsibility levies' was introduced, whereby farmers bore part of the cost of exporting. As a result, the net cost to the EC budget of grain exports was 2.192 billion ECU in 1987. Since then, it has fallen somewhat, and was 1.2 billion ECU in 1989. These measures all secured the agreement of the Council of Ministers. The Commission, however, has often felt that more dramatic action than the Council will support needs to be taken to reduce surpluses; hence it has resorted to a number of informal measures, including lengthening payment delays to producers, shortening the period of time in which wheat can be sold to the intervention authorities and tightening quality requirements for intervention purchases. The effect has been to cause modest reductions in producer prices.

Over the course of the 1980s, therefore, the European Community's CAP had a considerable impact on the world grain market, particularly on wheat. Its production grew, exceeding domestic requirements and creating a large export surplus. This has been a costly surplus, in terms of the Community's budget and economy and in terms of the world market. So great were these external costs that they became a bone of international contention under the GATT Uruguay Round. It remains to be seen whether the halting pace of reform within the EC is sufficient to reduce these costs to levels acceptable to other exporters and to the more reform minded of the Community's members.

Agricultural policy in the US

Policy in the United States has to respond to a different set of priorities. While farmers remain a powerful political pressure group, their influence on policy is mediated by the sheer size of the US agricultural sector. The US is simply not in the position to make an open-ended budget commitment to the farm sector. The importance of the US to the world grain market is evident in two ways in particular that are relevant to a discussion of policy. The country is the largest exporter of grain, and large exporters typically find themselves with special responsibilities, as the examples of Saudi Arabia in the oil market and Brazil in the coffee market attest. Leading exporters often find it is in their interest to act as swing suppliers or important stockholders, trying to ensure that prices do not fall too low. Secondly, world market prices for grain are established in the US, precisely because it is the key marginal supplier.

Throughout the post-war period, therefore, the US has occupied a special place in the grain market. Its policies towards the sector are designed to achieve the twin aims of providing some support to farm prices while not encouraging overproduction; such overproduction would either have to be exported at subsidized prices (threatening commercial export markets and posing a formidable budgetary problem) or accumulated by government stockholding. Obviously, this is a difficult balance to draw, and the US has frequently found itself holding large stocks of grain, the disposal of which has posed a problem. The key features of US grain policy work the same way for both wheat and coarse grains, although the actual price levels specified for different commodities are different.

Each year, the USDA sets a 'loan rate' for regulated commodities. This rate is the price at which a farmer, instead of selling his produce on the market, can use it as collateral to obtain a loan from the government. Thus, if the loan rate for wheat is $4.00 per bushel, a farmer can sign over his wheat to the Commodity Credit Corporation (CCC, the relevant government agency) and receive a loan which values his crop at $4.00 per bushel. This loan can be redeemed by the farmer, with only modest interest costs. So, if prices rise to $4.25/bushel, the farmer can reclaim his crop, sell it, repay the CCC for its loan and keep the difference (minus the small interest charges). Alternatively, after a certain time, he can default on the loan and forfeit the crop, in which case the grain has, effectively, been sold to the government for the loan rate. Through this mechanism, the government seeks to put a floor under prices, but there is no ceiling.[15]

The government has been careful, however, to try to avoid accumulating ever-larger stocks of grain. It does this by establishing supply controls. Under these controls, farmers who wish to take advantage of the CCC's loan programme must enrol in the supply control programme. This involves limiting the acreage planted to grain. The amount of acreage to be idled will vary from year to year, based on the assessment of supply/demand conditions made by the USDA. The farmer, therefore, has a choice: he can accept the

15 It is of course possible that, when prices are rising, sales of government stocks (accumulated during years of low prices) would have the effect of restraining the rise in prices.

acreage reduction and gain whatever comfort is provided by the government's safety net, or he can take his chances on the market. Clearly, there is a free-rider problem here. If enough farmers sign up for the acreage restrictions, the loan rate will put a floor under the market and even those farmers who have not signed up will, effectively, benefit from the floor under the market that the government provides. The recent history of grain policy in the US involves the attempt by the government to provide some support to farmers without accumulating burdensome stocks but, striking this balance has proved very difficult.

There are, however, a few refinements to policy that should be mentioned. In addition to the link between loan rates and acreage set-asides, which penalize farmers for not reducing their acreage, there are other programmes designed to pay farmers for taking land out of production. This began in 1956 with the Soil Bank, a programme geared at long term land conservation, and there have been a number of successor measures. Secondly, in the early 1970s, deficiency payments were introduced, whereby eligible producers received direct grants from the government to compensate them for any difference between the price actually realized on their crops and the 'target price' established by the government. Third, in the late 1970s the farmer-owned reserve was created. This set up subsidized on-farm storage of grain provided farmers agreed to hold the grain until prices reached predetermined 'release' levels.

Back in the 1960s, the US built up large stocks of grain because loan rates and supply restrictions did not lead to production levels that were equal to demand. In the early 1970s, the emergence of the USSR as an import market and some crop failures in various parts of the world caused the US stocks to be drawn down and prices to rise. These developments caused production in the US to increase sharply, and loan rates also went up. The 1970s were years of heady expansion of US agriculture. The US Farm Bill of 1981 reflected this optimism with high loan rates and modest acreage set-asides; and, reflecting the experience of the high-inflation 1970s, conditions were set that required loan rates to increase through 1985.

Unfortunately, the early 1980s were not as favourable to farmers as the 1970s had been. A worldwide recession harmed demand for grain, and a sharp rise in the value of the US dollar began to have a major impact on farmers. Since grain prices are denominated in dollars, and since US prices effectively set world market prices,[16] the rise in the dollar made wheat prices very attractive to farmers in other countries. Hence production in other countries began to rise as the demand for grain began to weaken. A sharp

16 The US is the major producer and exporter, and its producers are, in effect, the swing producers. Only in exceptional circumstances, therefore, will world market prices diverge from those in the US.

fall in US inflation made the prices mandated by the 1981 farm legislation look very high, and the two crop years 1980/1 and 1981/2 enjoyed good weather and therefore produced good crops. As a result, US stocks of grain began to rise.

To combat this rise, the government announced its Payment-in-Kind, or PIK programme. Under PIK, farmers would be rewarded for removing land from production by being 'paid' with grain from government stocks. This was designed to produce a one-off reduction in both production and government stocks without a dramatic effect on prices or farm incomes. More than 80 million acres were signed up under PIK, almost 20% of total US crop land, but the effects on wheat and maize were very different.

Ironically, wheat yields were very high on the reduced area of cultivated land, so the impact of the programme was muted. In the case of maize, however, the opposite happened. Poor weather in the mid-west led to sharply reduced yields on the acreage that was planted. These lower yields coupled with the PIK programme were responsible for the sharp fall in US coarse grain production, (Tables 4.6 and 4.7).

The gains from the stock reduction were short lived, however. Within two years, burdensome US surpluses had re-emerged and there was also the growing problem of the threat to US wheat exports posed by the EEC. In response to this, the 1985 Farm Bill continued to try to adjust the balance between prices and stock levels. The Secretary for Agriculture was given greater leeway to adjust loan rates to reflect supply and demand conditions, and this resulted in lower rates being set. There were also attempts to break the link between US and world market prices: an Export Enhancement Programme (EEP) was created whereby grains (and some other products) from government stockpiles were made available to merchants. The merchants could then add the government grain to commercial exports, allowing exporters to reduce the effective price per ton sold. (For example, an eligible importer could buy 100 tons at the market price and receive perhaps 20 tons free from the government stock pile. This effectively reduced the price by 20%.) Another important measure was that the gap between target prices and loan rates was widened so that farmers' incomes could be supported without supporting market prices. Finally, an enhanced land diversion programme was introduced, with both short and long term components. The Conservation Reserve Program (CRP) is a long term land conservation measure, and land entered into it cannot be cropped for ten years. By 1990, even though the 1988 drought caused a sharp reduction in grain stocks, some 45 million acres of US crop land had been entered into various set-aside programmes.

This huge unused agricultural productive capacity is a reflection of what was outlined in Tables 4.2 and 4.6; that US grain production, although variable, did not really grow in the 1980s. The US has acted as the key swing supplier, preferring to absorb the impact of production increases elsewhere rather than see prices fall to new lows. The US is not, however, particularly happy about the role it has adopted, and wishes to see the EC, in particular, take more active steps to link its domestic policies to world market conditions. Pressures on the federal budget also limit the capacity of the US to protect its farmers from world market conditions.

Grain policy - some summary observations

Agricultural policy in all countries has to balance conflicting interests: those of producers, consumers and taxpayers. It is further complicated by the fact that the interests of these groups are not internally homogeneous. The EC policy changed as the budgetary burden grew and it could no longer isolate itself completely from the world market. It continues, however, to oversee massive transfers from consumers to producers; transfers that are largely absent from the US policy framework. There are, perhaps, two important messages that should be taken from this brief review of policy factors. The first is that policy has a clear capacity to affect production. The production increase of the wheat yields in the EC has been made possible by the high prices paid to farmers. While the weather is obviously of vital importance in agriculture, policy can and does affect output for good or ill. Secondly, to the extent that every producing country seeks to insulate its farmers from world market conditions, the world market will become more and more an unstable, residual market. Since so much of the US's agricultural capacity is geared at exports and since it is so large a producer, its ability to insulate its farmers is limited. US grain policy, therefore, is far more likely to remain responsive to world market conditions than is policy anywhere else.

CHAPTER

5

Consumption

Some important features of grain consumption, particularly the dual role of grains as direct human food and as feed for animals have already been discussed. It can well be imagined that these two uses display rather different patterns. In Chapter 4, the longer term trend in the production of grain was outlined. No such long term historical perspective will be offered in this chapter, for the simple reason that, over the long term, production and consumption move together. Of course, in any given season the two may not be similar, and they will diverge sharply from time to time; but, over the long haul, they will be equal. The great growth in world production in the second half of the nineteenth century was obviously driven by an increase in demand.

One interesting historical question arises over the division of grain consumption between food and feed uses. Unfortunately, there are no satisfactory data in the long term pattern of consumption in these two markets to allow one to examine this over the period for which there are production data. It does seem likely that the nineteenth century explosion in demand and production was for direct human consumption. It is known that the production increase was overwhelmingly wheat, and that the use of wheat as an animal feed is comparatively recent. Moreover, consumer incomes in nineteenth century Britain were not large enough to allow large scale consumption of meat. The meats that were most widely consumed at the time, beef and sheepmeat, came from animals fed on grass rather than grain. The major revolution in livestock husbandry, which involved feeding animals large rations of grain (and other feedstuffs) to speed up their rate of weight gain, did not come until after the second world war. In other words, there are good reasons to believe that feeding grain to animals on the scale that is seen today is a recent phenomenon, but it is hard to quantify this with any degree of accuracy.

Although large amounts of wheat are used as animal feed and some coarse grains are used as human food, it is a useful simplification and not a terribly misleading one to imagine that wheat is used as direct human food whereas coarse grains are used as animal feed. This simplification helps to focus attention on the different determinants of demand. Meat (and other animal products such as milk and eggs) are more likely to be prominent in the diets of richer consumers. Since international trade in meat is quite limited in extent, one would, therefore, expect to see feed grain consumption concentrated in countries with high, or at least rapidly rising incomes. One would also expect to see consumption increase as incomes go up. It should not be surprising, however, to see a different pattern in the case of wheat. Consumers may well eat more meat as they get richer[1] but will they eat more bread? The answer is that they almost certainly will not. Of course, very poor consumers can increase their consumption levels, which is important in the recent history of the wheat market, but once moderate income levels have been achieved, the scope for sustained increases is limited.[2] The major factor causing wheat consumption to rise, therefore, is population increase.

All of which is to say that the income elasticities of wheat and coarse grains are different. The income elasticities of coarse grains are higher in most countries. This can be clearly seen in Table 5.1, where some sample elasticities are presented.

This table also shows the pronounced difference between developed and developing countries. Income elasticities of demand for wheat are very much higher in poor countries; indeed, they are negative in developed counties. This indicates that it is only population growth in developed

1 We have to be careful with this kind of claim. Very rich consumers may well eat less meat, as they become more concerned with the health consequences of meat eating: this has recently become an important factor in the US meat market. The relationship between income and meat consumption is not linear, in other words. There is little doubt, however, that as incomes rise from low to moderate levels, demand for meat (and hence for feed grains) rises.

2 Again, one has to be careful here. Wheat consumption in developing countries has been growing rapidly and, in part, this is the result of changes in the structure of the population. A peasant farmer in the countryside may rely on a range of staples, but probably does not eat much bread. If the family moves to the city, they are likely to become bread eaters.

Table 5.1 Income elasticities of demand for wheat and coarse grains in selected countries

	Wheat	**Coarse grains**
USA	−0.20	0.04
EC	−0.37	0.04
Canada	−0.24	0.04
USSR	−0.42	0.10
India	1.06	2.13
Pakistan	0.62	1.50
China	0.75	1.69

Source: W H Furtan et al, *Grain market outlook.*

countries that is allowing consumption in these countries to rise. The elasticities of demand for coarse grains are even higher still in developing countries. In China, the elasticity is 1.69, meaning that a 1% rise in income causes a 1.69% rise in the demand for coarse grains. The numbers are similarly high in other poor countries. This is no more than a reflection of the desire of people to eat more meat as soon as their incomes permit.

Both types of grain are price inelastic, but since wheat is more of a staple and coarse grains more of a luxury item, the price elasticity of wheat tends to be greater (in absolute value, that is: since price elasticities are negative numbers, it will normally be a smaller number) than that for coarse grains. Because of these different consumption patterns, it is useful to discuss wheat and coarse grains separately, although the feed use of wheat will be examined and the extent to which it undermines the simplistic division discussed above.

The consumption of wheat

Table 5.2 provides a summary overview of world wheat consumption. Over the 20 year period encompassed by the data in this table, world wheat consumption grew from 333 million tonnes to 536 million. Note, however, that the bulk of this rise came in the developing countries, whose consumption rose from 129 million to 290 million, more than doubling. The table also provides data on Asia (excluding Japan), the developing world's most populous continent. Consumption in developing Asian countries increased from 81 to 207 million tonnes, a much larger rise than that in the rest of the developing world. If one takes an even longer perspective, one finds a similar result. Over the period 1961–89, world wheat consumption grew at an annual

Table 5.2 Summary of world wheat consumption (million tonnes)

	1970	1989
Industrial countries	83.5	103.0
East Europe and USSR	121.1	145.4
Developing countries	129.0	290.9
Asia	81.2	207.5
World	333.7	536.8

Source: Economic Research Service, USDA.

average rate of 3.8%. Consumption in industrial countries grew at 1.6% per annum, whereas in developing countries the rate was 4.8%. This pattern simply reflects what was outlined earlier, the dependence of wheat demand on population growth.

This is even clearer if one looks at individual countries. In China, for example, wheat consumption increased from 34 million tonnes in 1970 to 100 million in 1989, an annual average increase of more than 7%. Over the longer period 1961–1989, Chinese consumption grew at an annual average rate of 6.5%. Similarly, Indian consumption grew by 4.8% per annum over this period, and the rate in Pakistan was 3.9%. Contrast this with EC's 1.2%, Japan's 1.4% and an industrial country average of 1.6%.

This pattern cannot be wholly explained by the different rates of population growth in the developed and developing worlds. In part, these gains in consumption are the result of economic gains by developing nations. It is interesting to note that the greatest gains have come in India and China, two of the poorest countries in the world. (Or at least countries with very large numbers of poor people and rapidly growing populations.) The capacity for poor people to increase their consumption of basic foodstuffs, such as bread, is considerable, since they are very often malnourished. It is in these circumstances that the earlier statement that rising incomes do not lead to increased wheat consumption obviously does not apply; and of course it is these consumption rises that are reflected in the high elasticities of demand for wheat seen in Table 5.1. China was also able to record impressive rates of economic growth in the 1980s, boosting consumer incomes and therefore allowing consumers to satisfy some of their pent up demand for grain.

One further interesting feature of wheat consumption is its comparative stability, at the world level. Wheat production, as seen in Chapter 4, can vary considerably from one year to the next, but it is normally the case that the bulk of these fluctuations are absorbed by stocks rather than consumption. What is true at the global level, however, is not necessarily true at the level of individual countries, as Table 5.3 illustrates.

Table 5.3 World wheat consumption by major country (million tonnes, July/June years)

	80/1	81/2	82/3	83/4	84/5	85/6	86/7	87/8	88/9	89/90
USA	21.3	23.1	24.7	30.2	31.3	28.6	32.5	29.5	26.5	27.0
EC-12	49.4	49.6	50.2	56.0	60.1	59.2	56.7	58.2	59.5	58.1
USSR	112.6	104.9	100.6	93.0	91.2	91.6	102.8	101.5	100.4	103.3
Turkey	12.8	13.4	13.6	13.7	13.6	13.7	14.0	14.0	14.1	15.0
Egypt	7.5	7.7	7.6	7.9	8.1	8.2	8.3	8.8	9.8	10.2
China	75.9	78.8	79.4	82.9	92.2	100.4	101.5	102.8	104.4	104.5
India	34.3	36.3	37.8	42.0	43.1	43.7	45.5	49.8	51.2	52.5
Pakistan	11.2	11.2	11.5	12.0	12.3	12.7	13.2	13.8	14.9	15.6
World	450.9	449.4	460.1	474.0	492.9	496.2	522.4	531.1	532.4	536.8

Source: Economic Research Service, USDA.

Table 5.3 presents a shorter run of data for some individual countries that are important consumers of wheat. For many years, the Soviet Union was the world's most important wheat consumer, but, as seen with wheat production, its position has recently come under threat from China. As little as ten years ago, the USSR's consumption was 30% greater, but this margin has been eroded and China has now established itself as the leading consumer. Note also that the other developing countries listed also show impressive growth in consumption.

Another interesting and important feature of the table is the volatility of consumption in some countries, notably the Soviet Union. Generally speaking, one would expect countries to be reluctant to allow their consumption to fluctuate by as much as has been the case in the USSR; international trade and stocks should allow these fluctuations to be smoothed out. The Soviet authorities have not followed this course, for a number of reasons: partly because the costs of importing enough grain would be enormous and partly because the heavy use of wheat as an animal feed in the USSR gives the authorities more flexibility than they would have if all wheat were human food.[3]

There is also a marked contrast between the pattern of consumption in the US and the EC. Consumption in the EC is not only much larger than that in the US (a disparity far greater than that in their respective populations), but has been much less volatile. To understand this, the use of wheat as an animal feed needs to be looked at.

Table 5.4 presents some data on the feed use of wheat. In overall terms, it

3 It is worth pointing out, however, that until the early 1970s, the Soviet authorities did not import grain to make up for domestic crop failures: they were absorbed in full by Soviet consumers, either directly in the form of bread shortages or indirectly through the availability of meat.

Table 5.4 Consumption of wheat as feed (million tonnes, July/June years)

	80/1	81/2	82/3	83/4	84/5	85/6	86/7	87/8	88/9	89/90
USA	1.6	3.6	5.3	10.2	11.0	7.7	10.9	7.6	4.2	4.3
EC-12	13.3	13.9	15.9	21.1	23.1	23.7	21.7	21.9	22.0	21.4
USSR	48.0	46.8	43.0	35.0	34.7	35.6	44.8	40.5	41.4	42.3
World	85.9	86.6	87.8	91.1	95.2	93.1	107.6	104.0	101.5	96.0

Source: Economic Research Service, USDA.

is clear that this is a major use of wheat: in recent years, about 20% of wheat consumption has been feed. One should not place too much emphasis on the global figures, however, since there is considerable uncertainty over the data in many countries. Moreover, it appears to be the case that small quantities of wheat are fed to animals almost everywhere, but this generally amounts to no more than a few percentage points of the local market. What is clear from the table is that feed use of wheat is heavily concentrated in few countries. The Soviet Union alone accounts for almost half of the world's feed use of wheat, a simple reflection of the fact that wheat is the highest yielding grain that can be grown on much of its land. Feed is also a major use of wheat in the European Community, accounting for roughly a quarter of world feed use of wheat and, more remarkably, over a third of total wheat consumption in the Community. This is a direct consequence of the Community's agricultural policy, which has stimulated production of wheat and restricted imports of competitive feedstuffs. This, of course, has resulted in greater use of wheat for feeding than in countries where feed users face world market prices for feedstuffs.

Feed use of wheat in the US, on the other hand, differs from that in the EC partly because it is lower (both absolutely and relative to total wheat consumption), and because it has been much more variable over the 1980s. Feed use jumped from less than two million tonnes at the start of the decade to eleven million tonnes in the middle, and then fell again to less than five million five years later. Year to year fluctuations have also been dramatic.

This pattern reflects nothing more than shifts in prices. Because of wheat's higher protein content, it is a valuable feedgrain. Farmers, however, are normally precluded from giving much of it to their animals because of its cost. When prices of wheat are low relative to the prices of other grains, there is obviously an incentive to use wheat as feed. Because of the different geographical conditions under which wheat and the major coarse grains are grown, and because of their different elasticities of demand, wheat prices can be high when coarse grain prices are low, and vice versa. Obviously, there is substitutability between the two, and this serves to limit the extent to which their prices can diverge: although it must also be acknowledged that, apart from the US, there are few countries where there is easy substitution between them. Nonetheless, it is important to bear in mind that the price relationship between wheat and coarse grains is not cast in concrete.

The consumption of coarse grains

Not surprisingly, the pattern of coarse grain consumption is somewhat different. The key difference arises because coarse grains are used primarily as an animal feed. The use of coarse grains as human food is very important in some regions of the world, notably Latin America and Africa. Overall, the US Department of Agriculture estimates that just under 70% of world coarse grain consumption is in the form of animal feed. In developed countries, food use of coarse grains is very limited: only about 1% of the US maize crop, for example, is sold to consumers as sweetcorn, and the proportion processed into popcorn is even smaller.

In recent years, industrial uses of maize have been growing: the two most important of these are making high fructose corn syrup (HFCS), a sugar substitute, and ethanol, a fuel. These uses are most important, and have been growing most rapidly in the United States. Table 5.5 shows data on the

Table 5.5 US utilization of maize (million bushels, September/August years)

	1985/6	1986/7	1987/8	1988/9	1989/90
Food and industrial	1,140	1,175	1,212	1,232	1,271
Seed	20	17	17	19	19
Feed	4,152	4,701	4,811	3,981	4,458
Total domestic use	5,312	5,893	6,041	5,232	5,748

Note: The 'feed' category is a residual; the 'food and industrial' category includes alcohol.

Source: Economic Research Service, USDA.

domestic uses of maize, the most important coarse grain, in the US. Again, the data are reported in bushels, reflecting the importance of this unit of measurement in the US markets.[4] It can be seen that feed use dominates the market, accounting for three quarters of total consumption. Unfortunately, the data do not allow a more detailed breakdown of the non-feed market, but most of it is in the manufacture of HFCS. The other important feature of

4 Recall that the conversion factor for bushels of maize into tonnes is 0.0254.

these data is that the non-feed market has been growing slowly but steadily; the volatility of consumption is caused by changes in feed consumption.

At the global level, there obviously is some variation in year to year human consumption of coarse grains, but overall it is safe to assert that the key features of the pattern of coarse grain consumption are determined by their use as animal feeds.

Broadly speaking, therefore, one would expect coarse grain consumption to be less affected by population and more affected by consumer incomes than wheat consumption. In other words, rich countries and those experiencing rapid economic growth are likely to occupy a more important place in the coarse grain market than in the wheat market. Tables 5.6 and 5.7 present data in a similar form to Tables 5.2 and 5.3, allowing direct comparison of consumption of the two types of grain. Table 5.6 presents some summary data on consumption of coarse grains. Note first of all that coarse grain consumption is very much larger than wheat consumption, a simple reflection of the fact that animals are rather inefficient converters of grain into human

Table 5.6 Summary of world coarse grain consumption (million tonnes)

	1970	1989
Industrial countries	265.6	304.1
East Europe and USSR	117.8	192.4
Developing countries	206.8	324.0
Asia	109.5	169.0
World	590.2	826.8

Source: Economic Research Service, USDA.

Table 5.7 World coarse grain consumption by major country (million tonnes, July/June years)

	80/1	81/2	82/3	83/4	84/5	85/6	86/7	87/8	88/9	89/90
USA	148.1	153.6	167.8	150.4	164.1	170.5	181.2	184.3	157.6	173.7
EC-12	95.1	93.2	90.6	86.2	86.6	83.1	79.4	78.6	79.8	79.2
USSR	99.5	98.3	100.7	111.7	113.8	113.4	114.9	122.6	120.9	127.8
Japan	19.2	19.2	19.0	20.8	21.3	21.4	21.8	22.5	21.9	22.3
Brazil	22.8	22.5	21.2	21.4	23.1	23.8	27.1	24.9	26.4	27.0
China	87.0	83.5	85.4	87.5	88.6	86.6	90.5	91.8	91.8	92.9
India	28.4	31.3	28.3	32.9	32.3	26.6	26.7	24.2	31.3	31.3
East Asian NICs	8.0	9.1	10.3	9.7	9.4	9.7	10.7	11.1	12.5	13.7
World	748.0	741.9	753.2	759.3	782.6	778.8	806.0	814.7	797.9	826.8

Note: The East Asian NICs are Hong Kong, Singapore, South Korea and Taiwan.

Source: Economic Research Service, USDA.

food: a pound of grain provides far more human nutrition if it is made into bread than if it is fed to an animal and thereby turned into a (small) quantity of meat. Over the 20 year period covered by the data in the table, world consumption grew from 590 to 826 million tonnes, at an annual average growth rate lower than that for wheat. Over the longer period 1960 to 1989, the average growth rate was 2.6%, compared to 3.1% for wheat.

Over this longer period, consumption in industrial countries grew at 1.6% per annum, the same rate as their consumption of wheat. The difference in overall performance is, therefore, accounted for by the developing countries, whose consumption of coarse grains grew at 3.2%, compared to 4.8% for wheat.

This overall pattern, however, conceals important variations from one country to the next, variations that are, to a large extent, the result of different economic performance. Within the industrial countries, for example, whose consumption overall has expanded only slowly, there has been dramatic growth in Japan's consumption, from 4.5 million tonnes in 1960 to 22.3 million in 1989, an average annual growth rate of 5.9%. Japan's growth was particularly rapid in the 1960s and 1970s, reflecting both swift growth in consumer incomes and a cultural shift as the population switched to a more western diet, involving greater meat consumption. This is still going on today, but has been largely completed.

A similar process has been occurring in the rapidly growing developing countries of East and South-East Asia. In terms of growth rates, the most impressive performer has been Thailand, whose consumption grew at an annual average rate of 21% over the 30 years from 1960 to 1989. Data on the four tigers of East Asia, Hong Kong, Singapore, Taiwan and South Korea are reported in Table 5.6, and the recent expansion in their consumption is clearly visible. In population terms they are small countries, and therefore do not appear to be particularly large consumers; but the growth in their consumption illustrates the importance of income growth for utilization of coarse grains. Economic growth in Brazil, though not as impressive as in many Asian developing countries, has been rapid enough to cause increases in coarse grain demand there, and without the depressing effects of the debt crisis in the 1980s, consumption would have grown much more rapidly. (Brazilian coarse grain consumption grew at more than 5% per year in the 1960s and 1970s.)

Another significant difference from the wheat market is the role of China and India. Recall that there was a rapid rise in wheat consumption in both of these countries, and that China had recently become the world's largest wheat consumer. In the case of coarse grains, these two have shown much less impressive growth. India's consumption is barely growing at all. China's is growing, but not as quickly as its wheat consumption. Expansion in meat consumption in China, however, which is widely expected in the years to the end of the century, will cause large increases in the demand for feedgrains.

There are two other features of Table 5.7 that deserve comment. The first is the volatility of consumption, both in individual countries and for the world as a whole. This volatility is much greater than it is in the case of wheat: note the sharp falls in US consumption in 1983 and 1988; in both cases, these were the result of shortfalls in the US crop in those years. In the later year, the impact of the US drought was large enough to cause a reduction in world consumption. Consumption in the Soviet Union has also been volatile, as is its consumption of wheat.

The second feature is the contraction in EC consumption of coarse grains. This is of course related to the expansion in feed use of wheat in the Community. The EC's farmers have been switching out of coarse grains (particularly barley) into wheat, and the price policy that discriminates against imported grains have given feed users a powerful incentive to use local wheat. The same policy has also encouraged a large switch out of grain feeding altogether. The EC is a huge importer of animal feedstuffs such as tapioca, corn gluten feed and meal (by-products of maize wet milling) and citrus pulp. These products share the important characteristic that they are not regulated by the CAP; they therefore are much cheaper sources of carbohydrate than grain. Imports of products such as these have become so large that the Community has felt the need to try to limit them. It has negotiated a deal with Thailand, the major tapioca producer, to limit exports and it has repeatedly tried to negotiate with the US over corn gluten products.

Grain consumption – some summary observations

Overall, grain consumption is far more stable than grain production, and as a result receives less attention from market analysts than production. In the short term, such volatility as there is in consumption is mostly caused by production changes; this can be clearly seen in the Soviet Union, for example. In open market economies, fluctuations in the production of one grain cause grain users to use another, relatively more abundant grain to the extent this is possible. Of course, the differences between the demand for grains as food and grains as feed mean that coarse grain consumption does not behave in exactly the same way as wheat consumption; but even in the coarse grain market, demand volatility in the short term is not particularly great.

Over the longer term, demand does change quite markedly, particularly for coarse grains. In this respect, interest is focused on developing countries. The process of economic growth tends to lead to sharp increases in grain consumption, for a number of reasons. Higher incomes and greater urbanization lead to an increasing demand for diversity in diets and often lead to the adoption of more 'western' eating habits. People joke about the global spread of US food companies such as McDonald's and Kentucky Fried Chicken, but this is only the tip of an iceberg of changing eating habits in developing countries. A detailed recent study of Korea[5] found a sharp movement away from rice and in favour of wheat as the economy grew in the 1970s and 1980s. Similar shifts are underway throughout East Asia. It is quite widely expected that Chinese consumption of coarse grains will grow rapidly in the future: in the late 1980s, the Chinese economy was growing at almost 10% per year: growing at a 10% rate, an economy doubles in size every seven years and, in the Chinese case, this would clearly lead to a great increase in meat consumption. Even at more modest economic growth rates, grain demand in China will expand sharply and the prospect of such increases in Chinese demand has led many grain executives to rub their hands in excitement. This is of obvious importance to the longer term outlook for the grain market, discussed in Part IV.

5 See Ingco, *Changes in food consumption patterns . . .*

CHAPTER

6

Exports and imports

World trade in grain is only a small proportion of total production. Indeed, much of the world's grain, far from entering the world market, does not even enter the traded market of the country in which it is grown: it is retained on-farm by the farmer to meet the food needs of the farm family or for feeding to livestock. Total exports of wheat amount to less than a quarter of world production, and exports of coarse grains fluctuate between 12 and 15% of production. In the case of rice, it should be noted that exports are only about 5% of production, reflecting the large amount of rice that is grown for the local market in Asian countries.

It is an important consequence of this that world trade patterns are not like those for many other commodities. While it is true that both the volume and the value of world trade in grains is huge in relation to other agricultural commodities, the pattern of trade is somewhat unusual. In part this springs from the importance that most countries place on their domestic production, but it also reflects the changed international political economy of grain commented on in Chapter 3. The switch in political power from grain importers to the largest grain exporter has inevitably been accompanied by changes in grain trade.

Among grain importers, there are three main types of country. At one extreme there are countries that are chronically food-deficit. Most of these are basically city-states, such as Hong Kong and Singapore, but one should also include large sections of the Middle-East (especially the Gulf states) and Japan. These countries' import requirements tend to be reasonably stable and predictable, since their demand tends to grow fairly steadily and their domestic production is not large enough to affect import needs very much.

At the other extreme there are countries whose import requirements are small and confined to specialist needs. The UK, for example, is now a net grain exporter, but does have a regular import trade. Its import needs range from white maize, mostly imported from South Africa to make breakfast cereal, to hard wheat, imported from Canada and the US for blending with the local crop to make a flour suitable for the kind of bread that consumers prefer. Again, the quantities imported by these countries tend to be reasonably stable from one year to the next.

In between these two extremes lie countries that meet a large proportion of their consumption needs from domestic harvests, but that rely on the world market to close the (often large) gap between production and consumption. Obviously, their import needs can vary considerably from one year to the next depending on the vagaries of domestic production.

These categories are no more than a useful guide to the determinants of import demand, and countries can and do move from one to another. India and Saudi Arabia both used to have substantial and regular import needs, but in both, domestic production has increased. India now buys only small amounts on the world market, and Saudi Arabia's supply/demand balance changed so much in the 1980s that, by the end of the decade, it formally requested that it be listed as an exporting, not an importing, signatory country of the IWA.

Similarly, on the export side, there are some countries that export small amounts when their domestic harvest is very good, but the export market is no more than a vent for this surplus production. There are only a few producers that produce directly and routinely for the export market. Obviously, the inherent variability in production means that export availabilities fluctuate from year to year, a volatility that would exist even if farmers were not responding to price signals as well, adjusting their production as best they can as prices rise and fall.

Even among these major producers it cannot always be asserted that export production is a viable, economically efficient industry. The EC is a major wheat exporter, a position it owes to the generous subsidies to its producers from its consumers and taxpayers. Although there are many wheat producers in Europe with costs low enough to compete effectively at world market prices, the total of EC production would be very much lower in the absence of subsidies. With domestic prices aligned to the world market, the EC would be at best a modest exporter of wheat. Hence the 'vent for surplus' is an important component of the world grain market.

Imports of grain are the difference between domestic consumption and domestic availability. To a certain extent, therefore, the story of grain imports can be derived from the information presented in the previous chapter about consumption. Over the long term, that is abstracting from the year to year swings in imports caused by variations in domestic harvests, importers' needs follow the trend in demand. Hence those countries where demand has expanded rapidly are, for the most part, the countries whose imports have grown rapidly. Industrial countries' imports of both wheat and coarse grains have been growing only modestly; only in Japan, where the switch to meat eating in the post-war period led to increased demand for feedgrains, did imports increase appreciably in the past three decades. In the developing countries, on the other hand, there is a different story. Over the period 1961-90, Mexican wheat imports grew at almost 20% per year, and coarse grain imports at a rate only slightly lower. Mexican imports are still not large, but they have been growing rapidly. In developing Asia, on the other hand, imports of coarse grains grew by over 10% per year in this 30 year period, and were almost 30 million tonnes by 1990, approximately one quarter of world imports.

Taken together, developing countries account for about 40% of world coarse grain imports and about two-thirds of world wheat imports. What is more, their increased import dependence is not confined to the rapidly growing economies of Asia. Africa now imports as much wheat as all the industrial countries combined (just under 19 million tonnes in 1990), and its imports have been growing at over 6% per year.

When one looks at long term growth rates of grain imports, however, one is struck most of all by developments in the USSR. Soviet imports of coarse grains grew at the startling annual average rate of 34% between 1961 and 1990; and imports of wheat grew at 14% per year. At the start of this period, the Soviet Union was a wheat exporter, providing small but significant quantities of high-quality hard wheat to the world market. (Indeed, the USSR is still listed as an exporting signatory country of the IWA). By the end of the 1980s, the Soviets were the largest wheat and coarse grain importers in the world. Of course, one must be careful when looking at the long term trends in volatile data, but Tables 6.1 and 6.2 show the importance of the USSR as an import market for both types of grain. Soviet wheat imports at the end of the 1980s were only half of those in mid-decade. In 1984/5, wheat imports peaked at 28 million tonnes, but even at half of this level five years later the USSR was the largest wheat import market.

There are three important features of the data in Table 6.1. The first is the high degree of volatility in imports in many major markets. The Soviet Union, whose imports went from 16 million tonnes to 28 million and then to 14 million in ten years is only the most dramatic example. China's imports almost doubled from the 1986/7 to the 1987/8 season, and Brazil's imports have also fluctuated by a large amount from season to season. One

Table 6.1 Wheat imports by major market (million tonnes, July/June years)

	80/1	81/2	82/3	83/4	84/5	85/6	86/7	87/8	88/9	89/90
USSR	16.0	20.3	20.8	20.5	28.1	16.5	16.0	21.5	15.5	14.0
EC-12	5.6	5.6	4.6	4.0	3.4	2.8	2.4	2.2	2.5	2.5
Japan	5.8	5.6	5.8	5.9	5.6	5.5	5.8	5.6	5.4	5.4
China	13.8	13.2	13.0	9.6	7.4	6.6	8.5	15.0	15.5	13.0
NICs	3.2	2.9	3.1	3.4	4.3	4.2	5.2	5.7	4.2	3.6
Brazil	3.9	4.4	4.0	4.2	4.7	2.2	2.8	1.3	1.1	1.8
Middle-East	6.5	6.9	6.7	11.0	11.2	8.7	9.5	11.3	10.3	16.0
Egypt	5.4	5.9	5.5	5.8	6.3	6.2	6.3	7.1	7.0	7.0
Algeria	2.3	2.3	2.5	2.8	2.8	2.8	3.4	3.8	4.2	4.3
India	0.0	2.0	2.5	3.3	0.7	0.0	0.0	0.0	2.1	0.0

Note: The NICs are Singapore, Taiwan, Hong Kong and the Republic of Korea. The Middle-East, in this table, is defined to comprise Turkey, Israel, Syria, Iran, Iraq, Jordan, Lebanon, Saudi Arabia and the Gulf States.

Source: Economic Research Service, USDA.

Table 6.2 Coarse grain imports by major market (million tonnes, October/September years)

	80/1	81/2	82/3	83/4	84/5	85/6	86/7	87/8	88/9	89/90
USSR	18.0	26.0	12.5	11.6	26.9	13.7	11.0	10.0	23.0	23.0
EC-12	19.7	18.5	14.3	12.2	9.5	5.5	3.1	5.0	3.4	4.5
Japan	18.9	18.3	18.7	20.5	20.7	21.5	21.4	22.3	21.4	21.8
China	0.8	1.3	2.7	0.2	0.1	0.7	2.2	0.6	0.2	1.1
NICs	7.1	8.7	9.4	10.4	8.4	8.9	10.0	10.6	11.4	12.7
Mexico	7.1	1.6	7.2	5.8	4.2	2.4	4.2	4.0	5.5	8.5
Middle-East	6.3	7.9	8.1	10.3	11.1	12.1	14.3	10.8	10.4	10.2

Note: The NICs are Singapore, Taiwan, Hong Kong and the Republic of Korea. The Middle-East, in this table, is defined to comprise Turkey, Israel, Syria, Iran, Iraq, Jordan, Lebanon, Saudi Arabia and the Gulf States.

Source: Economic Research Service, USDA.

of the most interesting examples is India, formerly a country with a serious grain deficit, where effective agricultural policies have ended this deficit and left the country with only a small, and in several recent years, a zero import requirement. Of course, the volatility of imports is simply the result of the combination of stable consumption and fluctuating domestic production, characteristics of the grain market that were reviewed in earlier chapters.

The second important feature is the growing importance of a number of developing countries, particularly those with large populations and reasonable economic performance. Again, this reflects the underlying dynamics of consumption, since most of these countries have very limited domestic production capacity. Take the Middle-East region, most of the countries in which are reasonably prosperous oil producers. Their imports more than doubled over the 1980s. Egyptian imports have also grown, again reflecting buoyant local demand. It is not clear that this level of imports is sustainable for two reasons. In the first place, the Egyptian government has boosted demand by subsidizing wheat consumption heavily, subsidies that helped to create a massive fiscal problem for the government and will have to be scaled back. Secondly, the large imports of the 1980s were helped by the low level of prices and the large subsidies available from the USA and the EC. Again, these are unlikely to be maintained and the Egyptians, unlike their wealthier neighbours, lack the kind of oil income that would allow them not to care about their food import bills.[1]

The third interesting feature of the table concerns the EC and Japan. Japan's imports have been remarkably stable, reflecting stability in consumption and the absence of significant domestic production. This indicates that the switch in consumer diets towards bread has been completed. EC imports are declining, but do not fluctuate very much. The EC is a substantial net exporter, so these imports can only be understood by recalling the important quality differences within the wheat market. EC production is overwhelmingly of soft wheat, and in many countries of the Community soft flours do not produce the kind of breads consumers prefer. Technical advances have allowed the extraction of gluten from soft wheat, gluten that can be added to a soft wheat flour and thereby produce a bread like one made from a hard flour. These advances have reduced, but not entirely eliminated, the need for imports of hard wheats from North America. Durum wheat is also imported into Italy for the production of pasta.

Table 6.2 presents data on coarse grain imports, data that reveal some similarities to and some differences from the wheat data. As in the case of wheat, there is considerable volatility in import levels, particularly in the case of the USSR. Soviet imports have quite often doubled or halved from one season to the next. Also note the steady decline in EC imports of coarse grains, which fell from almost 20 million tonnes at the start of the 1980s to under five million by the end of the decade. This reflects the growing wheat surplus of the Community and the increasing use of domestically produced wheat as a feedgrain, displacing imported coarse grains. As we saw earlier, EC production of coarse grains has actually declined slightly, because of the greater profitability of growing wheat.

More generally, however, it is possible to see, in the import data, the different pattern of consumption of coarse grains discussed in the previous chapter.

1 The fiscal position of importers is an important variable that should not be forgotten. Brazil and, indeed, a number of other Latin American states were large wheat importers in the 1970s and early 1980s. The debt crisis, and the associated domestic fiscal crisis, forced governments to cut consumer subsidies. These cuts, and increased production (especially in Brazil) caused import needs to shrink.

The large importers among the developing countries tend to be the richer countries: the oil states of the Middle-East and the growing East Asian 'tigers'. China's wheat imports grew in the 1980s and by the end of the decade China was rivaling the USSR as the largest import market. But China's coarse grain imports are tiny and, after rapid growth in the early 1980s, have fluctuated around the one million tonne mark with no discernible trend.

Note that Japan's imports are both large and rising, in contrast to the stability of wheat imports: this reflects the continuing growth in Japanese consumers' demands for meat. Japan competes with the Soviet Union for the position as leading importer, but the two could hardly be more different as import markets. Japan's imports fluctuate by no more than two million tonnes (about 10%) from one year to the next, whereas Soviet imports halved from 27 million tonnes to 13.7 million between 1984/5 and 1985/6, and more than doubled from ten million in 1987/8 to 23 million in 1988/9.

Tables 6.3 and 6.4 present data on exports of wheat and coarse grains. These tables also present the world totals. One would, of course, expect world exports to be equivalent to world imports; the inherent time lags in trading and the errors in reporting and recording systems mean that the two are never equal, but the differences are not large. Because there are fewer

Table 6.3 Wheat exports by major exporter (million tonnes, July/June years)

	80/1	**81/2**	**82/3**	**83/4**	**84/5**	**85/6**	**86/7**	**87/8**	**88/9**	**89/90**
USA	41.2	48.2	41.1	38.9	38.7	24.7	27.1	43.5	38.6	33.5
Canada	16.3	18.4	21.4	21.7	17.5	17.7	20.8	23.5	12.4	17.3
Argentina	3.8	3.6	9.8	7.8	9.4	4.3	4.4	3.7	4.0	5.9
EC-12	15.7	15.7	16.3	15.5	18.5	15.6	16.4	14.8	21.0	21.0
Australia	9.6	11.0	7.3	13.3	14.7	16.0	15.6	9.8	11.4	11.0
World	96.8	107.8	107.0	109.9	115.8	96.1	101.9	116.0	109.9	106.9

Source: Economic Research Service, USDA.

Table 6.4 Coarse grain exports by major exporter (million tonnes, October/September years)

	80/1	**81/2**	**82/3**	**83/4**	**84/5**	**85/6**	**86/7**	**87/8**	**88/9**	**89/90**
USA	70.1	59.5	52.5	56.1	56.1	36.1	45.8	52.1	61.2	69.7
Canada	4.8	7.5	6.5	6.6	3.6	4.6	7.1	5.2	3.4	4.5
Argentina	14.3	11.4	11.4	9.7	10.5	9.4	5.1	6.3	2.5	4.1
EC-12	5.9	4.0	4.2	4.3	8.5	8.1	6.3	8.5	10.8	8.5
South Africa	4.9	3.8	0.2	0.0	0.6	2.9	1.5	0.6	4.0	1.3
Thailand	2.4	3.5	2.3	3.1	3.5	3.9	3.1	0.8	1.6	1.2
World	118.8	109.5	96.4	104.3	111.8	94.6	96.6	96.3	106.5	110.9

Source: Economic Research Service, USDA.

exporters and because their data are thought to be more reliable, figures quoted for world trade are usually based on exports.

The data reveal the US as the key grain exporter, but there is a crucial difference between its position in the wheat market, on the one hand, and that in the coarse grain market on the other. The US share of wheat trade was over 40% in the early 1980s and had fallen to only a third by the end of the decade. The loss of market share was primarily to the EC, whose net exports rose by one third, from 15 million tonnes in 1980/1 to 21 million in 1989/90. Of course, there were fluctuations along the way. US exports fell to 25 million tonnes in 1985/6 and then recovered, but the clear trend is down (just as the clear trend of EC exports is up).

In the coarse grain market, however, the US market share is larger and has been more stable. The US exported 70 million tonnes out of a world total of 119 million in 1980/1, a 59% market share. In 1989/90, US exports were also 70 million tonnes, a 63% share of the world total of 111 million. Again, there were fluctuations along the way, but the overall position of the US is not under threat by any other producer. The EC's coarse grain exports have increased, but only modestly, and there is a huge gap between the US and the other exporters. It is also interesting to note that, among the top six exporters are nations (such as Thailand and South Africa) whose production is only a tiny proportion of world output.

In the case of both wheat and coarse grains, the 1980s saw a rather stagnant world market, with some fluctuations but no pronounced overall trend. In fact, this stability is more apparent than real, for there was much that was very volatile and changing during the decade. Understanding the major sources of instability and change is essential to understanding the dynamics of the world grain trade.

The Soviet Union

The trade data clearly show the influence of the Soviet Union on world trade patterns: both the level and the volatility of imports need attention. Obviously, the determinants of Soviet imports are of vital importance for anyone who wishes to get to grips with the grain market. So why do the Soviets import so much grain, and why is their import level so variable?

The shorthand answer to both questions is the remarkable inefficiency of Soviet agriculture. For all this inefficiency, however, it must be admitted that the overall quality of Soviet land is not very high. There is much excellent land, notably in the Ukraine, but the aggregate statistics are not encouraging. Sixty percent of the arable land is in areas where average temperatures are no higher then five degrees Celsius. Forty percent of the arable land receives less than 16 inches of annual rainfall, and is exposed to serious drought every three years, on average. Only 1% receives 28 inches of annual precipitation. To some extent, however, these poor overall figures reflect the policy of the Soviet leadership, notably under Khrushchev's New Lands policy, to expand grain cultivation to the east and north, bringing under the plough areas that were formerly grassland. This policy was itself the result of the failure of attempts to increase yields on the better land to the west and south.

Refer back to Tables 4.3 and 4.7 to see how grain yields in the Soviet Union are well below those in other major producers. The poor condition of much of the land is not a complete explanation of this: Canada's wheat yields are typically higher than the USSR's although Canada has far less grain land below the 49th parallel than the Soviet Union.

Soviet agriculture has also suffered from lack of investment. Until 1958, the agrarian sector was regarded as the prime source of capital for the development of industry and was discriminated against in the allocation of credit.

But these matters are niceties. The plain fact is that socialist agriculture, as practised almost everywhere but particularly as practised in the Soviet Union, has failed to keep pace with the growing demands placed on it; it has been an economic disaster. (Moreover, as is becoming increasingly clear, it has also been an environmental disaster, thanks to excessive application of pesticides and herbicides and poor land management practices.) Soviet farms are huge: the average size of a state farm in 1986 was 15,640 hectares, and average employment was 515. They are not specialized: over 99% of state farms keep both beef and dairy cattle. Labour productivity is well behind that in the industrial sector, and the famous story of Soviet tractor drivers, paid by the area ploughed, illustrates the gap between workers' incentives and desirable outcomes in terms of efficiency.

Interestingly, however, the most important inefficiencies in Soviet agriculture are not in grain production. They occur in post-harvest handling, storage and distribution and, most importantly, in the livestock sector. Feeding ratios in the Soviet Union are about double what they are in the West: that is, it takes about twice as much grain to produce a pound of meat in the USSR than in Europe or the US. Partly, this reflects distorted price ratios, which encourage farmers to feed grain to animals, but this is only part of the story of wholly inadequate incentives to use resources properly. Moreover, Soviet feeding practices do not seem to have improved since the 1960s.

Volatility in production is inherent in agriculture. This does not necessarily imply volatility in consumption, since countries can hold stocks; Soviet farming has never produced a large enough crop, however, to provide stocks for lean years. Until the early 1970s, the policy in the USSR was to constrain consumption to fluctuate '*pari passu*' with production, but riots in Poland in 1970 in response to bread shortages apparently led the Soviet authorities to fear similar disturbances if this policy were continued. Moreover, growth in meat demand was imposing a growing strain on the grain economy, largely because what grain could be produced was used so inefficiently. Hence, in the early 1970s the decision was made to supplement domestic production with imports.

The inefficiency of the agricultural system, therefore, is a good explanation of the need of the USSR to import large amounts of grain. Fluctuations in domestic harvests are a good explanation of fluctuations in import levels; and the main determinant of these production fluctuations is the weather, although there have, at times, been unexpected changes in the area planted to grain.

In the early and mid-1980s, when Soviet imports were particularly large, there were those who held there were two constraints on import levels: their port capacity and their access to money. It is doubtful that either effectively limited imports, although port logistics certainly were difficult for total import levels in excess of 40 million tonnes and it is true that the Soviets, who were normally cash customers for grain, often selling gold to finance their purchases, did use short term credit lines in the early 1980s. At that time, they experienced little difficulty in getting credit. Of course the steady growth in their indebtedness and the sharp deterioration in their economy since the late 1980s have changed this position.

There is one further element of uncertainty about Soviet imports, and that is their composition, in terms of type of grain and trade partner. The Soviet production shortfall is normally in feedgrains (including wheat, a large amount of which is fed to animals in the USSR). Yet they import large amounts of bread wheat. World price ratios between bread wheat and feedgrains are an important influence on this choice, but the geography of production and consumption within the country is also a factor. The inefficiencies of domestic transportation mean that bread wheat is often fed to animals in the countryside, while populations centres near the coast are supplied with imported bread wheat. The choice of trading partner is heavily influenced by political considerations: President Carter's restrictions on grain exports to the USSR following the invasion of Afghanistan made the Soviets reluctant to purchase large quantities in the US even after President Reagan lifted these restrictions, until bilateral relations had improved.
improved.

The People's Republic of China

Although China is a large grain importer, its grain economy is very different from that in the Soviet Union. Overall, Chinese agriculture is very efficient, particularly with respect to the use of land. The limited availability of arable land and the great population pressure have prevented the emergence of US style capital intensive farms and government policy appears to continue to place great emphasis on the role of agriculture in labour absorption. Grain is of central political importance in China, but this has not prevented the emergence of a strong dose of pragmatism in agricultural policy. Market based reforms, introduced in 1978, gave greater autonomy to peasant farmers in production decisions, and encouraged the production of meat to satisfy the large unfilled demand in urban centres. Chinese agriculture was, as a result, transformed, with rapid growth in grain production and, over the period 1978–85, a doubling of the quantity of meat produced. Moreover, the technical efficiency of Chinese meat production[2] is high. Feed conversion rates even for local breed hogs fed on less-than-perfect diets appear to be around 6:1, which, while not up to the standards of developed countries, is good. Some farmers, using hybrid animals, are achieving rates of around 5:1 not far off technical maxima.

The surge in meat demand since the economic liberalization in 1978 has led many to forecast dramatic growth in Chinese grain imports. The experience of Japan indicates that the income elasticity of feedgrain demand is around 0.8 until income reaches $3,000 per capita; an implied level of demand in China that could not be met by Chinese production in the absence of major technological breakthroughs. But there is a paradox here: while the growth in demand would appear to be in feedgrains, the bulk of Chinese imports are wheat. Indeed, in the early 1980s, China was a net exporter of feedgrains.

The resolution of this paradox lies in two factors. The first is the regional supply and demand balance. Generally speaking, the northern regions are grain surplus, whereas the west, and the south (and particularly the southeast) are grain deficit. The local transportation system is not capable of efficiently transporting grain along the required routes, and as a result one region exports while another imports. The second, more important factor is the importance the government attaches to the goal of self-sufficiency in grain. This is not an absolute goal, in that the government has been prepared to finance a certain volume of wheat imports to provide for the population's direct food needs. It seems clear, however, that the government is not

2 Something like 90% of China's meat is pork, a reflection of pronounced consumer preference. There is only limited production of other meats and dairy products.

willing to allow large scale imports of feedgrains to satisfy the domestic demand for meat. Apart from the financial and logistical constraints on imports, the authorities are anxious to avoid the pattern of import dependence that has emerged in the Soviet Union.

Hence Chinese imports, from one year to the next, are most easily explained with reference to the size of the domestic harvests and the availability of foreign exchange to finance grain imports. The political imperative to avoid import dependence also extends to the choice of trading partner. Chinese imports are quite widely sourced and a deliberate attempt to reduce imports from the US was made in the early 1980s, after a dispute over the access of Chinese textile exports to the American market.

The European Community

A third important change over the 1980s was the emergence of the EC as a substantial net exporter of grain. As recently as 1977/8, the EC was a net importer of almost 20 million tonnes of grain. It became a net exporter in the 1982/3 crop year and by the end of the 1980s was a net exporter of 25 million tonnes: a net impact on the world market of 45 million tonnes in little over ten years. The switch in the EC's net trade position in wheat has been slightly different from that in coarse grains. For coarse grains, the 1980s saw a sharp erosion of import levels and the emergence of a small net export trade, whereas in the case of wheat, of which the EC was already a net exporter by the start of the 1980s, net exports virtually doubled from ten million tonnes in 1980/1 to almost 20 by the end of the decade. This is important in understanding the impact of these changes on other exporters. Coarse grain exporters have lost markets in Europe, whereas wheat exporters have had to deal with an aggressively expanding new competitor in third markets.

Of course, from the economist's point of view, there is no difference between these two types of market erosion, but in the context of the political economy of the grain markets there is an important difference. Although the international framework for agricultural trade is being negotiated under the GATT, and things may therefore change, many countries have been reluctant to give up their ability to limit access to their agricultural markets. As a consequence, there was a widely accepted principle that policies to limit imports were less likely to incur the hostility of other producers than measures that had the effect of stimulating exports. Hence the EC's impact on the wheat market has received more attention than its impact on the coarse grain market.[3]

Exporters' responses

Taken together, these characteristics and changes in the market have posed major challenges to exporters. They have variable exportable surpluses, face volatile import demands in a total market that is growing only slowly and have had to deal with a dramatic change in the net trade position of the EC. This is to say nothing of prices, discussed in Chapter 7. Exporters (apart, that is, from the EC) have done one, or both, of two things.

In the first place, they have sought to guarantee their market shares through negotiating long term supply agreements with major importers. Although such agreements have been known in the grain trade for a long time, and have always been favoured by countries with public bodies in charge of grain exports (notably Australia and Canada[4]), they became very popular during the 1980s. Even the US, normally suspicious of such mechanisms, negotiated them with the Soviet Union and China.[5]

The shine has rather come off this mechanism, however, largely because the agreements have been shown to have little more than symbolic value. They are not enforceable, as was clearly demonstrated when, in the late 1980s, both China and the USSR failed to buy the minimum quantities specified in their agreements with the US. There was nothing the US could do about it. Similarly, the agreements provide little comfort to importers, since exporters who experience crop failures and do not have adequate stocks are in no position to meet their side of the bargain. These agreements, therefore, although perhaps valuable as public relations tools, have limited value in affecting trade flows.

The second strategy adopted by exporters has been to subsidize, a strategy designed to pass the effects of market volatility onto the shoulders of farmers in

3 Given the negotiations under the Uruguay Round, still continuing as this book was written, one has to be careful about such statements. One reason the EC's wheat trade position has attracted more attention is that the US has been able to build a bigger coalition to attack it. But the fundamental point stands, and, in fact, applies quite generally to trade, not only to agricultural products, even though the GATT limits countries' freedom of action in traded manufactured goods.

4 Not all grains are regulated by the Australian and Canadian Wheat Boards. Both bodies, however, have been enthusiastic users of long term supply agreements. In part this reflects these countries' heavy dependence on exports but volatile production levels.

5 The USDA originally sought an agreement with the USSR in order to dampen the effects on US markets of large but erratic purchases by the Soviet Union. Only later did the agreement come to be seen as a way of guaranteeing the US a share of the Soviet market. One important reason why the US has not embraced this marketing tool as enthusiastically as other exports may be that it does not need to. A recent study of trade flows revealed that importers tend to be more loyal to the US than to other exporters (see Wilson, Koo and Carter, *Importer loyalty . . .*).

another country. Export subsidies have always been an integral part of the EC's agricultural policy, but the growth of EC wheat exports in the 1980s entailed a rapid rise in expenditures on these subsidies. The financial capacity of the smaller wheat exporters (Canada, Australia and Argentina) was (and still is) far too limited to respond with similar programmes, although they did try to lower the effective price of their grain by such expedients as credit programmes backed by their governments. The US, however, not only had deep enough pockets to respond, it had the political will to do so. Amid the escalating rhetoric of a trade war, the US introduced a 'war chest' of subsidies, centred on the Export Enhancement Program (EEP) whereby importers who bought wheat (and selected other commodities) on commercial terms could supplement these purchases with free grain from government stocks. This obviously had the effect of reducing the price of grain to the importer. Although the intention when the programme was initiated was to confine it to a small number of countries where there was strong competition between US and EC grain, and thus target the subsidies to counter EC exports, it proved impossible so to limit it. The programme rapidly expanded to the point where almost all importers became eligible. Clearly, in the long run, such a policy was highly undesirable. One key aim of the US administration, however, was to make export subsidies extremely expensive for the EC and thus increase the budgetary pressure for reform of the CAP. Of course the US also suffered and the financial cost of this subsidy war, and its impact on other exporters, became one of the reasons why agricultural trade was so high on the agenda of the Uruguay Round of GATT talks.

CHAPTER

7

Prices

Long term price trends

In Chapter 1, evidence that grain prices in the Ancient World were considerably higher than they are today was discussed. Of course, it is very hard to compare prices meaningfully when there is no clear yardstick of comparison, but, even without making a formal comparison, there are good reasons to believe that prices are very much lower today, at least for consumers in industrialized countries. It is known that expenditures on food account for a much larger proportion of incomes the poorer people are. In a fundamental sense, prices are a reflection of purchasing power; if all some (poor) people can afford to buy is food, whereas other (rich) people can afford to buy food and a range of other goods, then the price of food the poor people face is very high relative to the price the rich people face. To the extent that people are richer now than they were in the past, food prices are lower; that is, incomes have risen faster than food prices.

The further back in history one goes, the harder it is to make specific comparisons of the prices of particular goods. In the case of grain, it is possible to go back a hundred years or so. As seen in earlier chapters, the opening up of the British grain market in the nineteenth century created the modern grain industry; one can, therefore, make a reasonably meaningful comparison of grain prices over this period. Identifying a particular series of prices, however, constrains the analyst somewhat. It turns out that the internally consistent price series available for the longest period of time is a series of season average farm gate prices received by US farmers. Having identified such a series, however, there is the further problem of inflation. The general price level has risen dramatically over the past century or so, and one needs to be able to look at prices in inflation-adjusted terms. This poses a further difficulty in the case of grains, which have been, over this time period, internationally traded commodities.

All of which is simply to say that any presentation of long term prices series should not be treated as though it were gospel. The data plotted in Fig. 7.1 should certainly be taken as providing only a general indication of prices since 1870. The data are the US season average farm gate prices, deflated by the US consumer price index into prices corresponding to the general price level of 1988. (The series was also deflated by the US GNP deflator, but no significant difference was observed.) Even with due allowance for all the difficulties with long term price series, Fig. 7.1 proves interesting.

In the first place, grain prices are very volatile. This volatility is particularly marked during the period prior to the First World War, when there were regular, sharp peaks in prices, followed by several years of more stable and lower prices. The size of the price movements is quite remarkable. It is quite common to see prices moving by 50% or more, in nominal terms, from one year to the next. It should also be borne in mind that these are season average prices, and there was a lot of intra-season volatility.

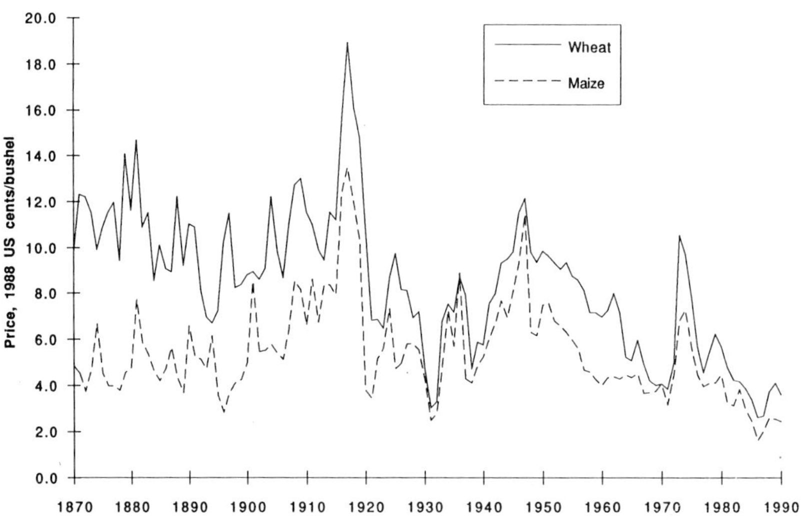

7.1 US wheat and maize prices (in 1988 cents per bushels).

There have of course been periods when prices have not been volatile. The 1950s and 1960s, for example, was a period when prices were not constant by any means, but they were falling in a rather steady and regular fashion. This relative stability was created by US policy in the period. The government was accumulating large stocks of grain, thanks to domestic overproduction, and these stocks were overhanging the market. US support prices were being reduced, and the data in the chart reflect these reductions in US support prices.

It has often been asserted that there has been a recent tendency for grain prices to become more volatile, due to the growing tendency for agricultural policy to try to insulate producers from world market conditions. This makes the world market more and more of a residual market, and therefore more volatile.[1] As one looks at Fig. 7.1, it is hard to attach much credence to this analysis. The 40 years or so before the First World War were very much years of free trade and only limited intervention by governments in the free movement of prices of agricultural goods. Certainly, on continental Europe there was some protectionism in response to the general depression of the 1880s, but in the UK and the US, grain markets were as free as they have ever been. Despite this, prices were extremely volatile. The period since 1970 only looks volatile in comparison to the rather staid decades of the 1950s and 1960s. Yet on the evidence of this chart, it is these decades that are the historical aberration.

Volatility is not necessarily a bad thing: price volatility does not imply volatility in incomes for producers (for example, if prices are lower because of an abundant crop, farmers will have more to sell, and whether their incomes rise or fall will depend on their specific situations[2]), nor does it imply equally large fluctuations in consumer prices (for example, if wheat is only a fifth of the cost of a loaf of bread, then a doubling of wheat prices will only put bread prices up by 20%). Moreover, to the extent that market institutions allow the risks of fluctuations in prices to be hedged, it is not at all clear that volatility is a bad thing. Certainly, the problem of uncertainty, which does create economic losses, should not be confused with volatility. Fluctuations

1 For a strong statement of this view, see Blandford, *Instability in world grain markets*.

2 It is, of course, true that individual farmers and consumers do badly out of volatility. The farmer whose crop is wiped out by drought cannot share in the happiness of his neighbour, whose good crop is sold at high prices. Poor consumers will suffer greatly if the price of a staple, such as bread, goes up by even a small amount. But these are particular problems, specific to these people's circumstances. They are really problems of bad luck or poverty, and they require government action. But they do not require that the government intervene in the grain market. The unlucky farmer can receive a grant, or crop insurance; the poor consumer an income supplement.

in price are the signals whereby information is sent to producers and consumers, encouraging them to adjust their behaviour to fit changing market circumstances. So observing that prices were especially volatile in the years before 1914 is not necessarily to make a negative comment about the period.

There are two other aspects of price volatility that are worthy of attention. Consider first the dramatic collapse in wheat prices between 1918 and 1932. In scarcely 15 years, wheat prices fell from a historic peak of $18 a bushel (in 1988 dollars) to a trough of only just over $2. This was the collapse that led to the widespread introduction of agricultural policies to protect farmers, an episode discussed in Chapter 3. Secondly, the figure shows the price peak of the early 1970s in a different perspective. Although it was a dramatic peak and was remarkable for coming after two rather quiet decades, it was in real terms well below previous peaks. Even at their peak, wheat prices were only a little higher than the trough they had reached in the mid-1890s.

The second important feature of the figure is the obvious decline in prices since 1870. Again, there are particular sub-periods during which there was no noticeable overall decline; in the years prior to the First World War, for example, there is a downward trend, but it is only modest. Over the years between 1920 and 1945 there was an upward drift to prices. Price movements in any one of these periods can be explained with reference to supply and demand conditions that are particular to the period. But it seems clear that, over the 100 year period covered by these data, there was a marked decline in real (i.e. inflation adjusted) grain prices. What accounts for this?

There is a closely related issue that has been much debated by economists. It has long been argued that the prices of commodities tend to decline relative to the prices of manufactures. Since most developing countries export primary commodities and import manufactured goods, a decline in the price of commodities relative to the price of manufactures would adversely affect the terms of trade of developing countries. This so-called 'Prebisch-Singer thesis' has been thoroughly investigated, and the balance of evidence is that there has indeed been a decline, although individual countries have been affected to varying degrees.[3] Thus the observed decline in grain prices should not come as too much of a surprise.[4] Moreover, many people who are concerned about the continued existence of hunger and malnutrition in

3 For a thorough discussion of the issue and the statistical evidence, see A I MacBean and D T Nguyen, *Commodity policies* . . .

4 Of course a decline in the price of commodities relative to that of manufactures is not the same thing as a decline in grain prices relative to the general price level (although they would be the same thing if there were only two goods, 'commodities' and 'manufactures'). But the two phenomena are clearly closely related.

many countries would argue that prices have not fallen far enough, since they are still beyond the purchasing power of the poor. The question remains, however, of the decline's causes, whether one views it as a good or bad thing.

There are two main reasons for seeing the decline in grain prices. The first is the growth in agricultural productivity. The Malthusian vision of the future, with population expanding more rapidly than agricultural productivity, has not (so far) proved to be an accurate depiction of the grain market. The simple reason is that Malthus underestimated the growth in productivity. It is true that productivity improvements have tended to come in waves, with periods of rapid advance followed by periods of stagnation. It is also true that in much of the period from 1870 to the First World War there was little in way of improvement. Indeed, it was widely held in the 1920s that a plateau in wheat yields had been reached and that continued increases in wheat production would only be possible through expanding the area under cultivation. Of course, this proved to be untrue, and there was a particularly rapid increase in productivity after 1945. The most spectacular results were achieved when selective breeding brought about the Green Revolution. The Green Revolution's promise for developing countries made crop breeding virtually front page news, but cross breeding and, in the case of maize, hybridization, had already produced a much quieter but very impressive improvement in yields, especially in North America and Europe. Indeed it was partly the increase in US yields that created problems for agricultural policy makers in the 1950s and 1960s.

Rapid technological innovation tends to cause price declines; this should not be a surprise to any purchaser of consumer electronics. Innovations tend to reduce both average and marginal costs, and this pushes down prices. (Since prices are [equal to] marginal costs.) But this is only the supply side of the equation. Conceivably, if demand could grow even more quickly than output, real prices would rise.

In the case of agricultural goods, demand conditions do not allow this. The amount of food a person can consume, while not fixed, is limited. People certainly can and do consume higher value foods as they get richer, but it is a well documented fact that, as people get richer, they spend less and less of each incremental unit of income on food. A 10% rise in a poor person's monthly income from $100 to $110 will produce a noticeable rise in the person's demand for food. But a richer person, whose monthly income goes up from $1,000 to $1,100, will not increase his consumption of food by as large an amount. Spending on food may go up, if he goes to more (or more expensive) restaurants, but the amount of food bought will not increase by very much. (Restaurateurs will see increased demand for their products; farmers will not.) Indeed, less bread may be eaten as the consumer gets richer.

Of course, the above explanation is a simplification, but it is correct in broad outline. In general, incomes will rise in line with the rate of productivity increase in the economy. If agricultural productivity keeps pace with overall productivity (in fact it has tended to outstrip it), then, if people's food consumption does not rise in line with their increases in income, agricultural prices will decline. For most people, getting richer means having more money to spend on other things; so it is no surprise to find that agricultural prices do decline.

Referring back to Fig. 7.1, these arguments do not apply with equal force to both wheat and maize. It is apparent that wheat prices have fallen a great deal more than maize prices over this period: wheat prices were roughly double maize prices in the closing decades of the last century, but this premium has eroded sharply, to the point where it is very modest.[5] Indeed, the downtrend in maize prices is a very modest one. There are three main reasons for this, one statistical, one substantive and one a quirk of agricultural policy.

The statistical reason is that prior to 1902, there was no effective way of removing the grains of maize from the cob. For this reason, almost all maize was fed on-farm or transported over very short distances. The presence of the cob made for uneconomic transportation. This makes farm gate prices for the period before 1902 a little difficult to compare with wheat prices; wheat was an internationally traded commodity in this period and farm gate prices reflected world market conditions. Careful inspection of the figure (and statistical analysis) shows that wheat and maize prices are much more closely correlated in this century than they were in the last. This is a reflection of the changed economics of maize after the invention of a technique to remove the grain from the cob cheaply, efficiently and with little damage.

The substantive reason is to do with the demand for maize (and for feedgrains as a whole). Feedgrain demand has expanded much more rapidly than demand for wheat. Consumer demand for meat (and other animal products) is much more income elastic than demand for bread. Moreover, although demand for meat is finite in the sense that the amount any individual can eat is limited, it takes so much grain to make a pound of meat that a small increase in meat demand has a large impact on demand for feedgrains. The growth in meat consumption in OECD nations since the 1920s has, therefore, resulted in a large increase in the demand for feedgrains. This has prevented the real price of these grains from falling as far as the real price of wheat. A more recent phenomenon, dating back to the 1970s, is the growth

5 The chart plots prices in dollars per bushel. Since a bushel of wheat contains 60 lbs whereas a bushel of maize contains 56 lbs, wheat prices per bushel would be higher even if prices per pound of grain were the same. In fact wheat enjoys a slight premium because of its protein content, but even this is eroding as changes in baking and animal feeding practices lead to shifts in demand for grain.

in the industrial uses of maize, particularly for the manufacture of the sugar substitute, high fructose corn syrup.

Thirdly, there is the quirk of agricultural policy. The price series plotted are farm gate prices; this price was chosen because of its internal consistency over such a long period of time. Yet the average prices farmers receive is a function of government policies as well as of market trends. Conceivably, a government willing to subsidize its agriculture very heavily could produce a situation in which farm gate prices rose or remained steady. Over the long term, the US has tried to run an agricultural policy that has not flown in the face of market realities, but there have been times, since the introduction of price support measures in the 1930s, when average price received by farmers have been above market prices; hence some of the data plotted in the chart reflect the prices established by the agricultural authorities, not those set by the market. Generally speaking, there has been a very close link between domestic US and world market prices, but it has been broken on occasion. To a certain extent, therefore, one could argue that the eroding premium enjoyed by wheat simply reflects the greater political power of the maize farmers in the agricultural policy formation process. Given the long run tendency for US prices to set world market prices, one cannot entirely dismiss this view. The persistence of the trend, however, makes one think that something more than policy is at work in the market for maize and wheat.

The fact that wheat is now so commonly used as a feedgrain suggests that no further erosion in the wheat premium will occur, although it is perhaps dangerous to offer such sweeping conclusions about the future.

Prices in the 1980s

The long term price chart (Fig. 7.1) shows that grain prices in the 1980s were at historical lows, in real terms. Figure 7.2 provides a closer look at the prices of wheat and maize in the 1980s. These prices are a little different from those plotted in Fig. 7.1, which were US farm gate prices; those in Fig. 7.2 are US export prices. They are monthly, not annual averages, and they also have not been deflated. But they provide an insight into some of the issues discussed in the previous section.

Consider, for example, the issue of volatility. By historical standards, the decade of the 1980s did not appear to be one characterized by a great deal of volatility. On closer inspection of the monthly data in Fig. 7.2, however, it is possible to see that prices were still volatile, despite their stability when compared to earlier decades. Over this ten year period, the maize price fluctuated between a low of just over $60 per tonne and a high of almost $150.

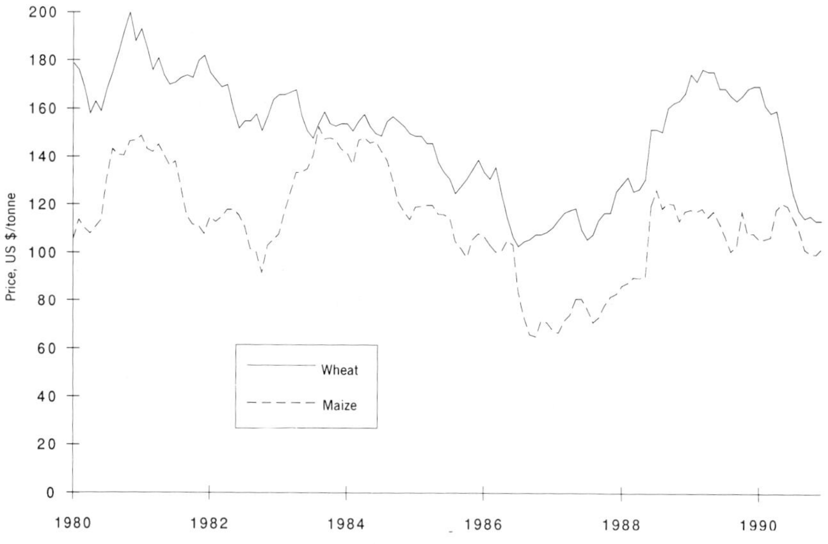

7.2 US wheat and maize export prices.

Wheat prices moved between $100 and $200 per tonne. Not all of these movements were gradual: it is not at all unusual to see prices moving by $10 per month. In percentage terms, these are large price moves.

Consider also the issue of the eroding premium for wheat. There have been several occasions in the recent past when wheat and maize prices have been almost the same; throughout the 1983/4 maize crop year, briefly in 1986 and again briefly in 1988.

The first of these episodes is by far the most important. 1983, it will be recalled from Chapter 4, was the year in which the USDA introduced its PIK programme in order to reduce the overhang of government controlled stocks. This coincided with unusually dry conditions in the Mid-West. As a result, the US maize crop was sharply reduced. The wheat crop was only marginally affected. The result of this combination of factors was a dramatic move in the wheat:maize price ratio. In late 1982, wheat prices were about 50% higher than maize prices. Barely nine months later, this premium had been entirely eroded, since maize prices had gone up by 50% and wheat prices had hardly moved. Naturally, the use of wheat as a feedgrain in the US increased during this crop year.

The recovery in maize production in the following year led to a fall in maize prices, and wheat regained its premium. The prospect of a large wheat harvest in 1986 led to a sharp fall in wheat prices early in 1986; since expectations about the wheat crop are formed earlier than those about the maize crop (because of the later planting/harvest schedule for maize), this led to a fall in the wheat premium. When it became clear that maize production was also going to be high, however, the maize price fell even further, even faster, opening up the premium once again.

The influence of the weather on prices can be seen again, very clearly, in the data for 1988. A hot, dry summer throughout North America created expectations of a much reduced crop, and prices rose sharply. The maize crop is more vulnerable to adverse weather than wheat. Recall that both winter and spring wheats are grown and that wheat is grown in a great range of locations. The concentration of maize production in a small geographical area makes the maize crop, and hence maize prices, particularly vulnerable to weather scares. Note that the price data tell us that the drought was not as bad as people had feared: maize prices gained on wheat prices, but after rising to a peak in July, fell back, whereas wheat prices continued to rise.

The other important feature of the chart is that it puts the 'weather market' of 1988 into perspective. Both wheat and maize prices reached their low points in 1986 and were rising when the drought hit in the summer of 1988. With the perspective of a few years, it is apparent that the impact of the drought was no more than to cause a small upward movement in what was already an upward trend.

It has been argued that the fundamental explanation of developments in the grains (and other commodity) markets in the 1980s is to be found in the markets for foreign exchange. Certainly, the movement in the international value of the dollar is an important factor. The dollar began appreciating against other currencies in October 1979, when the Federal Reserve enacted a major policy change in order to combat inflation more effectively. This led to higher US interest rates and an appreciation in the dollar. The election of Ronald Reagan and the economic policy he followed (of fiscal expansion along with monetary restraint, leading to a budget deficit that exceeded the supply of domestic savings and therefore had to be financed by inflows of foreign capital) led to further appreciation. This was significant for the grains markets because world market grain prices are denominated in dollars. Consider the position of the Argentine wheat farmer. If the Argentine currency falls in value relative to the dollar, then the local currency profits of the Argentine wheat farmer have gone up, even though nothing has happened to world market wheat prices.[6] Obviously, Argentine production will expand. This certainly did happen in the early years of the 1980s and the rise in production outside the US inevitably put downward pressure on prices. One of the prime beneficiaries of the increase in the dollar

6 It turns out that the impact of a change in the value of the dollar on commodity prices is quite complex, and depends on the elasticities of supply and demand in the US and the rest of the world. For a fuller treatment of this issue, see Commonwealth Secretariat, *Variable exchange rates and trading on commodity markets*.

was the EC; the burgeoning expense of the export subsidies made necessary by the CAP was limited by rise in local currency grain prices.

In February 1985, however, the finance ministers of the industrialized nations met in New York and fashioned what became known as the Plaza Accord. Named after the hotel in which they met, this Accord provided for co-ordinated intervention by the major central banks to drive down the dollar. In this, great success was achieved: the dollar declined virtually monotonically until the end of 1987 (the Deutsche Mark, for example rose from $0.29 to $0.64 over this period). The sharp shift in the trend of the dollar naturally led to a compensating trend in the dollar prices of commodities. To a certain extent, therefore, the rise in grain prices that began in early 1986 can be seen as a response to the fall in the value of the dollar that had begun a year earlier.

Up to this point, a single wheat price and a single coarse grain price has been looked at to represent movements in the market as a whole. Is this justified?

Interrelationships among wheat prices

Figure 7.3 provides a closer look at wheat prices in the 1980s. The figure plots the export prices of standard grades of wheat from four major exporters. It is immediately apparent that the prices do move very closely together.

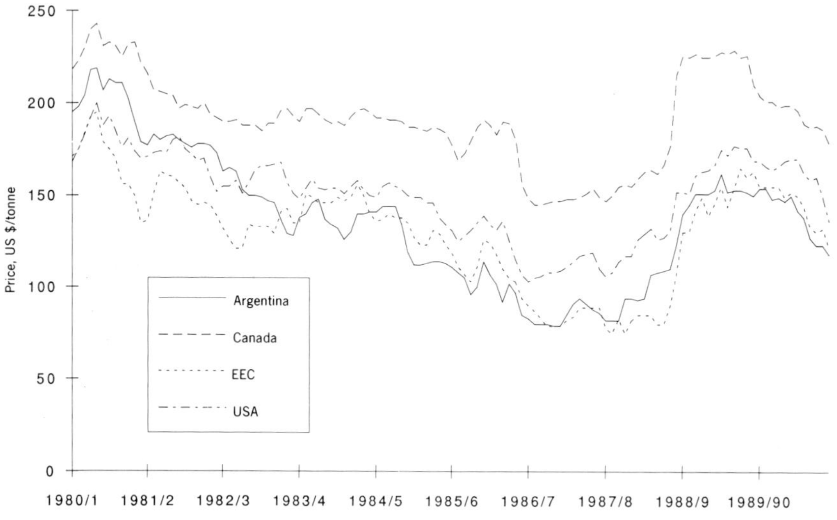

7.3 Wheat export prices.

Indeed, export prices of Australian Standard White Wheat are not plotted, for the simple reason that this grade is an almost perfect substitute for the grade of US wheat presented. As a result the two prices follow each other so closely that the chart becomes hard to read. The steady erosion of prices in the first half of the decade can be clearly seen, as can the sharp recovery in 1988 and the decline in 1989. But the data need closer study.

In the first place, it is easy to see the premium enjoyed by Canadian wheat. This is simply a protein premium; the grade of Canadian wheat whose price is plotted here is a standard Canadian grade, but conditions on the Canadian prairies favour the production of high protein wheats. The protein premium can be seen to vary; it was quite low in 1981, and quite large in 1985. The cause of this variation can be found on the supply side. Fluctuations in the Canadian crop and in the protein content of the wheat crops elsewhere affect the availability of protein, and millers, who generally like to use a blend of flours with a constant protein content to ensure the uniformity of their products, respond to these changes in availability by altering their purchases.

Over the longer term, changes in technology that allow first the extraction of gluten from low protein wheats (leaving the carbohydrate content of the grain for the starch processing industry) and then the addition of this gluten to a low protein flour, thus mimicking a flour from a high protein wheat, have been expected to result in the erosion of the protein premium enjoyed by the hard, spring wheats grown in Canada and the Northern US. In fact, as Fig. 7.3 makes clear, this does not appear to have happened.

Another interesting feature of the chart is the pattern of competition between the EC and Argentina. As seen in Chapter 6, the expansion of EC exports in the 1980s has affected the US most, in that the US has seen its market share eroded most. In order to be able to sell its wheat on the market, EC export prices have to be below those of the US, but it has long been a piece of folk wisdom that Argentine wheat is the cheapest on the world market. The chart does not appear to confirm this view.

In fact, the reason for the high relative price of Argentine wheat in the early 1980s is to bc found in the political realm. The embargo imposed by President Carter on US grain exports to the USSR enjoyed reluctant support among most other exporters, but Argentina refused to accede to the US request that it not make up the shortfall created by the US withholding supplies. As a result, Argentine wheat jumped in price on the world market, and it was not until late 1982 that it dropped below US wheat. In the period since 1984, the prices of Argentine and EC wheat have moved very closely.

Finally, Fig. 7.3 shows even more clearly a point that was made about Fig. 7.2 in connection with the impact of the 1988 drought and its impact on prices. Canadian wheat prices are the most interesting in this regard. After falling quite sharply in the early months of 1986, prices stabilized and began to move up slowly but steadily. By May 1988 they were almost $30 above the low point of 1986. In June, prices jumped by $39, greater than the entire increase over the previous two years. The drought damage to the Canadian crop was sufficient to maintain prices at this higher level throughout the 1988/9 crop year. In the US, where drought damage was less severe, prices advanced less sharply (and were actually stable in the weeks when Canadian prices were rising so quickly) but continued to climb after Canadian prices had found their level.

Interrelationships among coarse grain prices

There is a wide range of coarse grains traded internationally in large quantities, and an even wider range of grains that are consumed overwhelmingly within national markets. The most important of the traded coarse grains is maize. As seen in Chapter 4, the US is by far the largest coarse grain exporter. When looking at the interrelationships among coarse grains, therefore, it makes sense to look at the US market. Within the US, the three most important coarse grains are maize, sorghum and barley.

Figure 7.4 plots US prices of these three grains over the 1980s. These are domestic market prices, primarily because not enough barley is exported from the US to provide a good export price.[7] To the extent that feedgrains are used as a source of carbohydrate in animal diets, they are good, if not perfect substitutes, and one should expect their prices to be very closely correlated. Figure 7.4 confirms this. The maize and sorghum prices are so closely related that it is hard to tell them apart at many points on the chart. But although the barley price does follow the other two reasonably closely, it does sometimes diverge. Differences are particularly noticeable in 1983, 1986 and 1988. What can account for this?

The most important factor is that barley has an important market apart from animal feed, in malting. Although the two markets are quite separate in that different grades of barley are used for malting and for feed, there are times when one market affects the other. In particular, it is possible to use malting barley for feed, when market conditions allow. A second factor is

7 The three prices are as follows: Maize, number 2 yellow, Omaha; Sorghum, number 2 yellow, Kansas City; Barley, number 2 or better feed, Minneapolis to January 1987, Duluth from March 1987. This change in the basis of the barley price, reflecting a change made by the USDA, accounts for the discontinuity in the chart. These prices are very closely correlated with export prices: apart from short term disturbances that are too small to be picked up in monthly average data, the maize price in Omaha differs from that in the Gulf ports only by the transportation costs.

7.4 Coarse grain prices.

that barley is grown in quite different regions of the US from maize and sorghum. In 1983, the increases in maize and sorghum prices that were followed only with a lag by barley were the result of the droughts that threatened the maize (and sorghum) crops in those years. The barley market was a little slow in responding.

To the extent that a particular grain has supply and demand conditions different from those of maize, its price can be expected to diverge. A good example is provided by oats. The market for oats is somewhat unusual for two reasons. In the first place, they are not as dense as other grains and, as a result, their volume:weight ratio is unfavourable for long distance transportation. Hence local prices of oats can fluctuate more than other grains in response to purely local factors. Secondly, it is widely believed that horses have a preference for oats and wealthy owners of thoroughbreds are naturally anxious to keep their beasts happy. In so far as they do not buy grain simply as a carbohydrate source, but attach value to the type of grain, they can affect the price of oats. Hence it often happens that, when other coarse grain prices are weak, the price of oats is higher than its nutritional value would suggest is appropriate. This reflects the market for horses' feed.

The determinants of prices

There are many important factors that have an influence on grain prices through the supply of and demand for grain. Oil prices, for example, affect farmers' production costs (because of their influence on fertilizer prices and the costs of the energy farmers need for their farm machinery) and affect the demand for grain by shifting income between oil producers and oil consumers. Agricultural policy affects prices by giving farmers explicit or implicit guarantees about the prices they receive and by affecting the prices at which consumers can buy grain. World economic conditions affect grain prices through their impact on consumer incomes. Monetary factors also have an influence; interest rates are an important element in production costs, and changing exchange rates can also affect both supplies and demands. The purpose of this section, however, is not to review all these issues, but to look at a simple relationship that is useful in understanding price movements and is frequently used as the basis of commodity price forecasts. This relationship is the stock/consumption ratio.

The stock/consumption ratio provides an easy way of measuring the balance between supply and demand. Consumption is obviously a direct measure of demand, and the level of stocks provides a measure of the ability of supply to meet that demand. In principal, the ratio can be measured at any time of the year, but when production is seasonal (as it obviously is with grains), a measurement more frequent than annual would need seasonal adjustment. Grain stocks are much higher immediately after the harvest than immediately before, but, under normal conditions and if the size of the crop is well known, there will be no dramatic price consequence of harvest. For this reason, in the grain markets it is normal to measure the stock/consumption ratio at the end of the crop year. In some commodity markets (for example sugar) it is usually the case that analysts look at the global ratio; intuitively, this makes a great deal of sense. With grains, however, the global ratio is not very meaningful; partly because data on some countries' stocks are very poor or not available (the Soviet Union and China, for example) and partly because the different crop years that apply in different countries make it difficult to aggregate stock levels at any single point in the year. Instead, the ratio in the US is more commonly used.

This is less misleading than it might at first appear, since US prices are effectively world market prices and since the US is the major grain exporting nation. To a large extent, therefore, it absorbs fluctuations in world market conditions in its own stock levels.

Figures 7.5 and 7.6 plot prices and the stock/consumption ratios for wheat and maize in the US market. In each case, the ratio is multiplied by a constant in order to produce a number of a similar order of magnitude to the price. The close, inverse relationship between the two can be seen clearly. When stocks are high relative to consumption, prices are low. Conversely, when stocks are low relative to consumption, prices rise. To this extent, the figures provide no more than confirmation of one's intuition.

It is also apparent that this is not a perfect, linear relationship and one

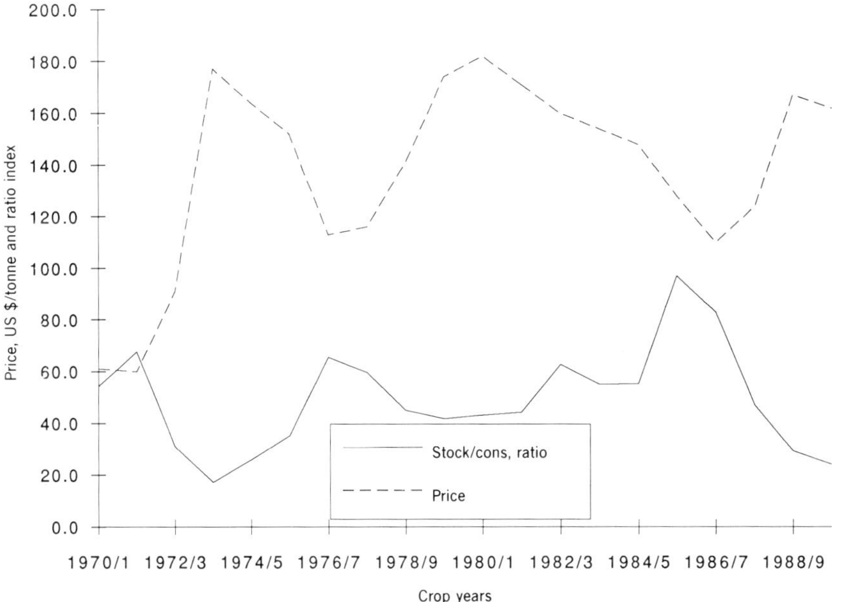

7.5 Wheat price and stock/consumption ratio.

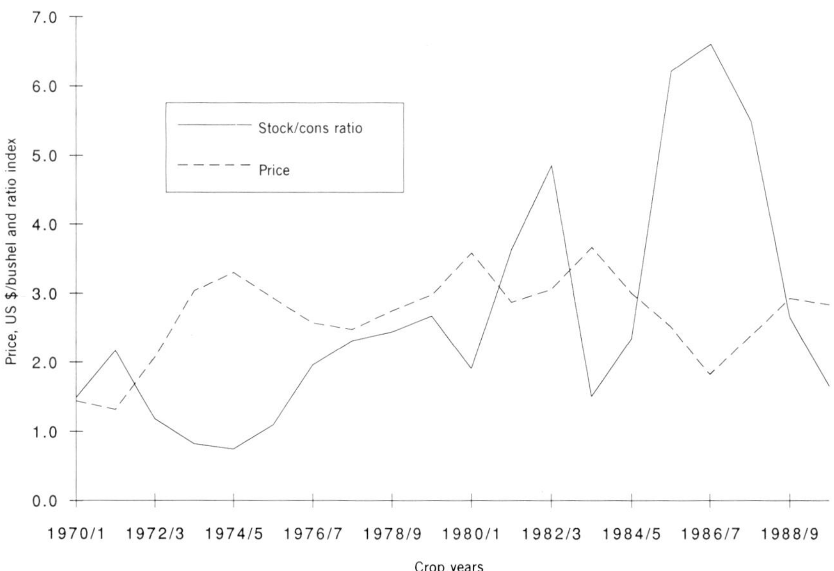

7.6 Maize prices and stock/consumption ratio.

should not expect it to be so. When stocks are low, one would expect to see a more-than-proportionate rise in prices, and when stocks are high, there will be a limit below which prices will not fall. There are also a number of factors that are not captured by this simple relationship. In the first place, it matters who holds stocks.

Private agents hold stocks partly to meet their expected physical needs, and partly as a form of insurance against unforeseen shortages.[8] When governments hold stocks as a way of meeting announced policy objectives, and there are predetermined and publicly known rules for stock disposal, the incentive for private stock holding is reduced, since private actors know government stocks will be released if the market gets tight. When there is over-production, it is often the case that government stocks rise, and private traders take advantage of the situation to reduce their stock levels. Hence, for detailed price analysis, one needs to know in greater detail who owns (or rather who controls) the stocks.

Secondly, one has to be careful about expectations. The data plotted in Figures 7.5 and 7.6 are season average prices and the end-season stock/consumption ratio (defined as end-period stocks divided by total period consumption). Obviously, early in the season, the end-period stock/consumption ratio is not known, and the movement of prices throughout the season will affect consumption (and therefore the end-period stock/consumption ratio). Throughout the season, prices are moving in response to developments in the supply/demand balance and thus to expectations about the end-period stock/consumption ratio. To the extent that expectations are not fulfilled, the relationship between the season average price and the stock/consumption ratio will be affected.

Thirdly, the data in the figures reflect US market conditions. As was argued above, these are a good proxy for world market conditions, but there are times when conditions in the rest of the world will affect US prices without having a major effect on either US stocks or US exports. When this occurs, US prices move by more than appears to be warranted by the change in the US stock/consumption ratio.

Despite these obvious drawbacks, the stock/consumption ratio is a useful tool for measuring swings in the supply/demand balance for grains, and is surprisingly good when used as a statistical predictor of prices. For further details see Chapter 10.

8 They may also hold stocks as a form of speculation, to benefit from possible rises in prices.

PART

III

The institutions of trade

CHAPTER

8

From farmer to consumer: the marketing chain

Key problems in marketing grain

Conceptually, moving grain from the farm to the consumer's table is a straightforward task. Take wheat for example; all that happens to it is that it is harvested, threshed, and ground into flour. The flour is mixed to dough and baked into bread and the bread is ready for the consumer. The entire operation used to take place (and still does in many countries) within the same village. Of course, the marketing chain is more complex in the case of feedgrains and meat, but even so the whole operation is nowhere near as complex as the marketing chain for a manufactured consumer product. Indeed, for the large proportion of the world's feedgrains that is kept on the farm and fed to the farmer's livestock, and therefore does not enter the formal market at all, one would be justified in saying the marketing chain is extremely short.

The job that is done by the marketing chain can be described simply in terms of managing the physical movement of grain from the farmer's field to the consumer's table. In this chapter only the first part of this chain will be looked at: from the farm gate to the processor (the flour miller, for example). The marketing of bread is rather different; it is a consumer product, not a commodity, so one should expect to see more differences than similarities.

There is, however, more to grain marketing than the physical shipment from the farm to the mill. A marketing chain is best understood as a process whereby information is transmitted between producers and consumers. As this information flows, so the market adjusts available supplies and demands, both spatially (moving grain from surplus to deficit areas), temporally (storing grain in times of plenty to guarantee supplies in times of dearth) and in terms of quality (adjusting premiums and discounts for different grades and grains).

Although the co-ordination of grain and information flow is, conceptually, a simple task, it should be noted that a large number of countries have not been able to do a good job of it. Examples of failure in marketing chains are legion. In developing countries, a major area of research has been how to limit post-harvest losses of food; problems such as quality degradation, insect and rodent infestation and spoilage are extremely serious and are marketing failures in that what gets to the consumer is neither as much nor as good as the farmer grows. The Soviet Union also has a notoriously inefficient marketing system, plagued by post-harvest losses and a distribution system that is incapable of delivering what consumers want when they want it. The winter of 1990/1 brought this home quite forcefully to the European and American public, when the West sent food aid to the USSR despite a good harvest. The problems the country faced that winter were distribution, not production problems.

Why is it that, in many countries, it has proved so difficult to establish good marketing chains? To understand this, the conditions marketing chains have to deal with have to be examined. Marketing systems for grain have to deal with three fundamentally important factors, two of which, production volatility and seasonality, are inherent to the grain market, and one of which, specialization and internationalization, although not inherent, is a distinctive feature of the modern grain market.

Production volatility

The inherent uncertainty about agricultural production makes prices volatile if they are free to move. In a planned economy, prices are set, and production volatility is passed through to consumers by shortages, or by allowing queues to get longer or shorter. Planning always made less sense for agriculture than it did for other products; and recent events in the Soviet Union and Eastern Europe have made the analysis of planned agricultural marketing systems of no more than academic interest. But even within a market economy, the degree of price volatility can vary; prices for grains do not vary very much in the European Community, for example. (Although such a policy is not without cost, as seen in earlier chapters.) Of course, changing prices are necessary to convey information to consumers and producers; a higher price is a signal to consumers to use less and to farmers to produce more. It is very difficult for administered price regimes to send the right signals to producers and consumers. But the important point is that a marketing system has to find a way to allow prices to adjust, to send signals along the chain.

Seasonality

The problem posed by seasonality can be simply stated. Grain is produced in one season, but is consumed throughout the year. A marketing system has to ensure that grain is available throughout the year. At its most simple, this means that the economy has to provide storage facilities, so that the production can be put into stocks and drawn down over the course of the year. Grain can be stored in all kinds of facilities, some of which are very simple. Simple granaries are commonly used in many developing countries. The typical modern way to store grain, however, is in what is called an elevator in the US and a silo in the UK. These facilities, in addition to storing grain, are often equipped to load, dry and discharge grain as well.

Storage will only be provided if the assets employed in storage earn a return, and the need to provide a return to the providers of storage has important implications for prices. Simply put, it gives seasonality to grain prices. Even in the EC, where grain prices are administered by the authorities to conform with the CAP, there is a monthly storage increment by which prices rise throughout the season to cover the costs of storage. To compensate stock holders for the loss arising from the drop in prices at the start of the season, the EC also makes a carry over payment to allow grain to be stored from one season to the next.

A persistent problem in many countries has been the underprovision of storage facilities in which grain can be kept without deteriorating. In some countries (notably Australia), permanent storage is underprovided because the grain crop is highly variable from year to year, thanks to the weather, and, if there were enough storage for the largest crops, it would stand idle for the years between bumper crops. The Australians have solved this problem by developing short term, low cost, temporary storage facilities. Argentina also lacks storage, with the result that it is under great pressure to export its crops as quickly as possible after harvest. In other countries, good grain crops are often simply left to rot.

Why would storage be underprovided given the fundamental economics of seasonal production and constant consumption? In Australia, it is simply because of the variability of the crop and the reluctance of private investors to build facilities that will stand idle much of the time. Almost everywhere else, however, it is for one (or both) of two reasons. One is that agricultural policy constrains the variability of grain prices, making it impossible for storage providers to earn a return. The second is that the agricultural marketing system is a part of the government (whether directly or indirectly) and investment in grain storage has to be weighed by the authorities against all the other competing demands on public investment funds. This second factor is particularly important in Africa, although the deregulation and demonopolization of agricultural marketing has been a noticeable feature of the very recent past in many African countries.[1]

The conclusion is inescapable; even in something as basic, fundamental to a seasonally produced crop and apparently simple as the provision of storage facilities, a number of countries have failed to develop good marketing systems.

Specialization and internationalization

The third important feature of the grain market is its increased specialization and the large role of international trade. A grain economy in which a farmer simply transports his grain to the nearest town, where a miller stores it, grinds it and sells the flour to a local baker has a less complex marketing task than a modern grain economy in which both food and feed grains are shipped many thousands of miles from farmer to consumer. The complexities are all the greater when one recalls other important features of grain. In the first place, it is bulky and expensive to transport. Even on the most efficient grain route in the world, with large ships running between the ports of New Orleans and Rotterdam, transportation costs routinely account for between 5 and 7% of the landed price of grain: on a route involving smaller ships and less efficient ports, a figure of between 10 and 12% would be more common. Secondly, production is inherently variable in quantity and quality. A user (a baker, say) who wants to produce a reasonably uniform product at as low a price as possible will need to alter the blend of raw materials as the quantity, quality and price of wheats from different regions or countries alter.

It was argued in Chapter 2 that the modern grain economy really emerged in the nineteenth century when Britain opened up to imports and began to import wheat from all over the world. British users of grain (essentially millers and bakers engaged in producing bread for British consumers) were faced with exactly the same problems that face modern grain buyers: uncertain harvests, volatile prices and expensive transportation. They built

1 For a review of the disasters of grain marketing in Africa, see Hopcraft, *Grain marketing policies and institutions in Africa*.

their mills and bakeries in or close to ports to keep shipping costs as low as possible.[2]

Moreover, the farmers who were dependent on exporting to the UK also faced difficult problems: dependence on a market a long way away, lack of control over marketing opportunities and volatile prices. Not surprisingly, it was at this same time that modern marketing institutions began to emerge. Among these institutions were the large grain companies who now dominate the world's trade in grain, and futures markets, discussed in Chapters 9 and 10.

There is a tremendous variety of marketing arrangements in the world: there are pronounced differences in the extent to which the market sets grain prices, in the extent to which the trade is controlled by public institutions and in the extent to which agricultural policy absorbs risk or passes it on to different participants in the market. Generally speaking, marketing systems in which virtually everything is controlled by public institutions or regulations work less well; for the simple reason that public institutions are less flexible in responding to the rapid changes in prices that inevitably occur. Regulations often succeed merely in setting up barriers that private traders find ways around; the numerous scandals in recent years concerning the Common Agricultural Policy are eloquent testimony to this. On the other hand, there is a good case for public authorities to take an active role in providing quality assurance (through grading standards, for example) and in ensuring that market prices are adequately arrived at and publicized.

Within the confines of this chapter, it is not possible to review and assess the great variety of marketing systems in use around the world. In keeping with the book's focus on the global market, the marketing system in the US, the largest grain exporter will be looked at, and the way in which international grain freight is organized.

Grain marketing in the United States

Grain marketing in the US is, to all intents and purposes, left to the free market. Of course there are important public interventions in the market, notably in the form of government price supports, and these certainly do affect the marketing chain. But it is by far the most free system of any of the

2 One interesting consequence of the UK's accession to the EC, and therefore of the CAP, has been the growth of its cereal production to the point where it is a net exporter. As a result, less and less British bread is made from imported wheat, and bakers, increasingly reliant on domestic supplies, have been moving their bakeries away from ports and closer to the inland areas where the wheat is grown. The clear motivation is to reduce transportation costs for grain.

major grain producing and consuming nations. The US is also the largest grain exporter, so it is particularly important to understand its marketing system. The system in the US is essentially the same for all the major grains, and for soybeans. Everything said here about grain applies almost without qualification to both maize (and the other major traded feedgrains) and wheat.[3]

Even in the US, where virtually all agriculture is commercialized, a large proportion of the maize crop is not sold by the farmer; rather, it is kept on the farm for feeding to livestock (typically hogs, but also cattle). In recent years, roughly 30% of maize has been retained on-farm by farmers. The decision to retain grain on-farm is itself a marketing decision; many farmers keep livestock as a form of diversification. Since hogs (or cattle) can be viewed simply as processed grain, farmers who keep animals can choose to sell maize directly in the form of grain, or indirectly in the form of meat. Since very little wheat is retained on-farm for feeding, however, it is important to concentrate on following the grain that is sold onto the market.

The first step in the marketing chain is when the grain is moved from the farm to a local elevator. The farmer may sell the grain to the elevator owner, or he may simply store it there (in which case he will, of course, be charged a fee). The elevator owner obviously wants to maximize the use of storage capacity, and will therefore compete on the prices he offers to farmers. The smallest elevator facilities are between 50,000 and 300,000 bushels in size; country elevators are rarely more than one million bushels. There has in recent years been growth in on-farm storage facilities, but it is rarely economic for farmers to invest in large elevators, for two reasons. In the first place, there are considerable economies of size in storing grain.[4] Secondly, the advent of mechanical shelling of maize in the field has resulted in farmers harvesting maize when the moisture content is quite high, in the 22–28% range. This results in much less damage to the grain, but is much higher than the 14% or so that is the moisture level necessary for extended storage. As a result, artificial drying is necessary, and this can often be done more cheaply at a local elevator.

Given the economies of size in storage, why are any small facilities still in operation? This is because of the high assembly costs of grain. Transporting grain from the farm to the elevator is expensive (since it is normally done by

3 The principal difference between wheat and maize is that wheat is grown over a more dispersed geographical area. Hence the network of marketing facilities is rather more spread out.

4 A 4 million bushel elevator can store grain for about half the cost per bushel of a 350,000 bushel elevator. However the turnover rate of grain has a large effect on costs; more rapid turnover of grain reduces unit costs because fixed costs can be spread over more bushels.

truck). Moreover, it is normal to keep grain as close as possible to the point of production until it has a final market. But it is true that, the further one goes down the marketing chain, the larger are the storage facilities. At sub-terminal markets, elevators hold several million bushels, and at terminal markets and export loading points, large elevators may hold up to 50 million bushels or more.

A terminal market is a large, central facility where buyers and sellers congregate, where there are storage facilities and where there is a process of public price discovery. The grain prices quoted in Chapter 7 were, in many cases, terminal market prices (e.g. the maize price at Omaha, or the barley price at Duluth). These markets are simply the organized outgrowth of the coffee shops and bars where farmers, dealers, merchants and traders used to meet to transact business. As the size of the shipments gets larger, it is more likely that the grain will be transported by rail or by barge. Waterborne transport is the cheapest, but it is (obviously) not always an available option.

It was mentioned earlier that the farmer may sell his grain to the local elevator or may simply rent storage space there (usually because he expects prices will rise). Country elevators normally work on a posted price basis; that is, they establish a price they are willing to pay for grain, and a farmer can simply telephone his local elevators and get a price quotation. The elevator owner can also offer farmers the same terms that he gets on his sales, and there are three main techniques used to set a price for the grain that elevators sell to terminal or sub-terminal markets.

Consignment

The first is the consignment method. Under this system, the grain is consigned to a merchant at a terminal market. The merchant does not take ownership of the grain but simply agrees to act as the owner's agent and try to get the best possible price for the grain. In return for this, the merchant gets a commission. Often the merchant also acts as a source of credit for the elevator owner, extending part of the value of the grain consigned. Under the consignment system, the elevator operator is exposed to the risk that prices will decline while the grain is being shipped to the terminal market. Protection against this risk can be achieved, however, by hedging in the futures market, see Chapter 10.

On-track/to-arrive

The second is the on-track, or to-arrive method. This method of pricing transfers the price risk from the seller to the buyer, because the buyer offers the elevator owner a price for grain 'to arrive' at a terminal market within a certain number of days. This kind of business is often attractive to elevator operators, partly because it is less risky and partly because they often feel that large traders in the terminal markets have a better feel for the market and so can offer a better price.

Futures

The third method is to price against the futures market. This means selling the grain for a price at a fixed relation to the relevant futures market quotation. For example, grain might be sold for 'eight cents under Chicago', meaning for eight cents less than the price that day on the Chicago futures market. (Normally the nearest contract month is used, but grain can also be sold many months in advance by this technique, using the futures price as a way of writing a forward contract.) This type of sale makes hedging easy, but it is risky if the actual basis (that is, the difference between the futures price and the actual cash price) varies. If this happens, the elevator operator could be left with grain that is bought at eight cents under Chicago but which can only be sold at ten cents under Chicago. Basis relations tend to be stable if one looks at them over the longer term, but they can vary from week to week.

Who are the people who buy grain from farmers? Local elevator owners are often small companies, who own no more than a handful of facilities. Some are farmer co-operatives, and others are owned by large trading and agribusiness companies. Terminal market operators are sometimes independent traders, sometimes agents of processors (e.g. flour companies and bakeries) and sometimes agents of grain trading companies. The grain trading companies will be discussed in Chapter 9.

The US grain trading system differs from its system for trading other agricultural products in two main ways. First, it gives a greater role to futures markets. Only soybeans, among other farm products, use futures markets to the same extent in marketing. Secondly, there is much less direct contracting. In many farm product markets, processors set up contracts with farmers under which they agree to buy the whole of the farmer's crop. This type of marketing was popularized by vegetable processing companies, but is now used quite widely. Among the grains, only popcorn and seed maize are marketed this way, and they are a tiny proportion of the crop.

Grain marketing by public bodies

How does the US system differ from those in other exporters? In brief, it is the one with the least involvement of public authorities. In the EC, although there is extensive price control, the bulk of the actual marketing of grain is in private hands. The risks that private operators face are limited by the price regulations, but the system operates in a way not dissimilar from that in the US, constrained only by the key policies of the CAP. There are even grain futures markets in the UK, and they are used by the grain trade even though the degree of price volatility permitted by the CAP is modest.[5] In Australia and Canada, most grain marketing is done by public bodies, the Australian and Canadian Wheat Boards (the AWB and the CWB). Although they do differ in important respects, the following brief description of the CWB will serve to illustrate the important features of a Board dominated system.

Canadian Wheat-Board (CWB)

The CWB was initially established in 1935 to bring a measure of national control to wheat exporting from Canada; farmers had the political influence effectively to nationalize the grain trading system. As a result, the CWB now has extensive control over every aspect of the grain marketing channel in Canada. (Although the Board is free to use private companies as contractors and its regulatory powers only extend to wheat, oats and barley.) The CWB is a Crown Corporation, self-financing, charged with the responsibility of marketing as much grain as possible at the best possible price, while ensuring equitable access for all producers to the market. To do this, it runs a delivery quota scheme to smooth out deliveries and co-ordinate them to market demands. In advance of the crop year, the CWB establishes an initial price for the grain it will accept: this price reflects the Board's assessment of market conditions, and also effectively provides a floor to the market since there is a government guarantee behind this price. (The government guarantees the loans the CWB contracts to make the payments.) Once the season is over, and the Board has sold all the delivered grain, it makes an additional payment to farmers if the total realized returns from the crop are greater than those implied by the initial payment. (If the realized returns are lower than the amount implied by the initial payment, the government makes up the difference.)

The CWB also makes direct export sales. As a quasi-governmental institution, it is able to conclude government to government sales, and to arrange official

5 Of course, even small movements in prices can mean large swings in margins (and hence profits) in the grain trade, where margins are generally very low.

credit for up to three years. But all its sales are on an in-store or FOB basis.

The CWB does much more than establish prices and sell grain overseas. It also organizes grain deliveries, schedules handling and transportation in conjunction with the railroads and inland waterway carriers. Canada's transportation infrastructure imposes some important constraints on the Board: the port of Churchill, on the Hudson Bay, is only open for shipping for about ten weeks in the summer, and the St Lawrence Seaway ports are also iced up throughout the winter. Access to the West Coast ports, Vancouver and Prince Rupert, is restricted by the rail network; regulated rail freight rates through the 'Crow's Nest' pass through the Rockies eroded the return to transport, and resulted, in the 1970s, in a deteriorating rail network. Changes were made to the system in 1983, and the network began to improve; but managing this constrained system is not the easiest of tasks.

In pursuit of its objective to give all producers equal market access, the CWB also effectively controls the domestic transportation network. Grain marketing in Canada, therefore, is to a very large extent the work of the CWB.

It is a consequence of this system that there is no price uncertainty within the season for Canadian grain farmers. Their returns are uncertain, of course, because they do not find out about the second payment (usually small) for a long time, but they do not have to worry about when in the season to deliver their grain. This is a sharp contrast to the position in the US. Studies have found, however, that year-to-year (or rather season-to-season) volatility is just the same in the two countries; since Canadian grain has to be sold on the world market (where its price follows the prices of other grains, as seen in Chapter 7) and since it is not within the power of the CWB to insulate farmers from the ups and down of the world market, prices can fluctuate quite sharply from one season to the next.

The international marketing of grain

To a large extent, the actual logistics of moving grain from the export port to the consumer (the flour mill, for example) are handled by the big grain trading companies, see Chapter 9. Fundamentally, moving grain internationally is not much different from shipping it across a large country like the US. A buyer enters a contract to buy grain, and a trading company effects the shipment, whether the buyer is in Minneapolis, Moscow or Algiers. Of course, there are exchange rates to worry about when export is involved, but the co-ordination of loading facilities, ships and so on is perhaps a little more complex but not different in kind from domestic shipment.

Very often, the overseas buyer acts just like a domestic buyer; i.e. by contacting different traders, searching for a good price, then accepting an offer. In many countries, however, a more normal procedure is to call a tender. Tenders are widely publicized and are invitations to supply certain quantities of grain according to a specified schedule. The buyer evaluates the responses to the tender, and places his order. The procedure is no more than a more formal way of calling around traders. Competitive tendering is very common in many industries; many international financial institutions insist that it be used in the projects they are financing, for example. Although it is a very widely employed practice (almost all developing country grain importers use it, for example) it is rather inefficient for grain. This inefficiency arises simply because of the volatility of grain prices. Prices of capital goods do not vary by much from day to day, so tenders can be evaluated at the slow pace of developing country institutions without large costs. But grain prices do vary in the short term. The companies who submit bids at tenders are aware of the risk that they run in offering to hold prices for business when the business may not be transacted for several weeks, and they will compensate for this risk by charging a higher price than they would otherwise. It would be easy to use futures markets to overcome this inefficiency (see Chapter 10), but remarkably few developing countries choose to do so.

Grain shipped internationally is normally shipped under one of the standard contracts commonly in use. The most common are the North American Export Grain Association (NAEGA) number 2 contract, and the Grain and Feed Trade Association (GAFTA) contracts. NAEGA is based in Washington DC and GAFTA in London. GAFTA has a number of different contracts, depending primarily on whether the export sale includes insurance and freight. These standardized contracts (which are revised every five years or so to reflect changing practices in the trade) are rather long, with clauses covering quantity, quality, delivery, price, payment terms, and arbitration procedures, alongside numerous other clauses. Arbitration is normally done in New York or London. Precisely because these are standard contracts that are in very wide use, they are the preferred way of conducting international trade. Disputes are quite rare.

The quality terms are of interest. Some exporters, notably Australia, Canada and the US, have grain grading schemes that provide a measure of confidence to the buyer that the quality of grain will be constant from one year to the next. The grades and the criteria used in assigning them are published. In other countries, however, grain is often sold on a 'faq', or 'fair average quality' basis, where the only guarantee is that the shipment is representative of the overall quality of the crop.

The grain freight market

One final piece of the marketing puzzle is the grain freight market. This is an important link in the chain because grain is a bulky, low value commodity. Transportation costs therefore account for a substantial part of the landed price. Another reason for wanting to know something about the market is that the proportion of the landed price of grain that is accounted for by ocean freight is variable, because the prices of both grain and freight are volatile and not closely correlated.

On a trade route between efficient ports used by large vessels (e.g. New Orleans to Rotterdam), ocean freight varies between 3% and 15% of the landed price of grain; on a less efficient route (to a typical developing country importer, for example), ocean freight will rarely be below 10%, and may be as high as 20% of the landed price. This is higher than the average for world trade as a whole; based on balance of payments statistics, freight accounts for about 7% of the landed price of all goods.

The cycles of grain prices and freight rates are not well correlated for an obvious reason. Grain price cycles are driven by the weather, by agricultural policy and by general economic developments. Grain freight rates are set in the market for freight, which has its own supply/demand balance. The balance reflects the supply of shipping (itself heavily influenced by the subsidies paid by governments anxious to keep their national shipyards in operation) and the demand for freight (determined principally by the general level of economic activity). Grain is only one element in the freight market, and, since modern vessels can switch from one cargo to another (thanks in part to modern cleaning techniques), swings in the markets for commodities as diverse as oil, iron ore and phosphates can affect the price at which grain can be shipped internationally.

The grain freight market does differ from those for other dry bulk commodities, however, in one crucial respect. Trade in the other major commodities is highly concentrated geographically. This has allowed the development of very large vessels, dedicated to a particular commodity and often dedicated to a particular trade route. The geographical dispersal of grain trade, with such a large number of importers with variable import needs, has prevented such a development occurring in grain. The comparative stability of trade in other dry bulk goods means that there is a market for long term shipping contracts, whereas in grain, not only are cargoes typically smaller, a higher proportion have their prices fixed in the spot market.

Most vessels employed in the grain market are tramp steamers, that is vessels that are available for hire on any route (provided they can gain access to the loading and discharging ports). Very little grain is carried on scheduled cargo vessels. Tramp steamers can be hired on any one of a number of standard terms (as in the case of the grain itself, standardized contract forms are available). Long term leases are also available, but most grain vessels are chartered on a 'voyage charter' basis. Agreements between vessel owners and users are called charters. Under a time charter, a vessel is hired for an agreed period of time, irrespective of where it may go, whereas under a voyage charter, a vessel is hired to undertake a specific journey (which may involve more than one port at loading and discharge).

There is a futures market for freight rates; traded in London, it is an index of a number of the largest trade routes on which time and voyage charters are used. But the physical market is not an organized terminal market, even though there is an active spot market centred on London. The great majority of the world's freight business is conducted over an informal network that links owners, customers and international brokers. Brokers are often very specialized in a small number of commodities, or even a small number of trade routes. Ship brokering is generally reckoned to be a competitive business, and the grain freight market, probably more so than any other freight market, is considered to be extremely competitive.

What determines freight rates? Clearly, the overall supply/demand balance for vessels determines the level of rates, but there are still considerable variations in what is paid from one route to another. There are three main considerations that need to be borne in mind. In the first place, there are economies of scale in shipping. Unit costs are lower in big vessels; both loading/unloading and per mile costs are lower. Secondly, the speed at which a vessel can be loaded and unloaded (i.e. the efficiency of a port) is very important. Finally, the probability that a vessel can secure a further cargo (a 'backhaul') will also affect the price. To serve an out of the way port, from which a vessel will need to leave empty and travel a long way to pick up its next cargo, an owner will demand a higher fee. For all these reasons, developing countries tend to pay much higher freight charges than do developed countries.

Grain marketing - some summary observations

Moving grain from farmers to consumers assumes great importance in the world market primarily because of the instability of key prices. Grain prices move sharply up and down, and premiums and discounts for different grades also move quickly. Grain freight prices also move up and down quickly, reflecting developments in the freight market as a whole. This price instability imposes risks on farmers, traders merchants and consumers, and different marketing chains represent different ways of passing these risks from one party to another. In the US, farmers and futures market speculators bear a lot of the risk; but in other countries, the risks are allocated differently.

Marketing systems are also important because of the manifest failures of the marketing chains in many countries, notably in the Soviet Union and in Africa. The fact that so many countries have made such a mess of grain marketing should make one appreciate the efficiency of the systems that do work. If establishing a good marketing chain were easy, more countries would have one.

CHAPTER

9

Grain trade: the key players

Ever since the 'Great Grain Robbery' of the early 1970s, it has been impossible to discuss the grain trade without raising the issue of the small number of large, multinational trading companies that move almost all of the grain that is traded internationally. The debate over these companies lacks focus and clarity and there are numerous misconceptions about what these companies actually do and whether their activities are a legitimate cause for public concern. To a large extent, the issue rose to prominence because of general public feelings of hostility towards multinational, or transnational, corporations (MNCs or TNCs). Since the big grain trading companies are TNCs, the argument runs, they must be a bad thing. To this general hostility was added a special piquancy because these TNCs appear to 'control' the world market not for any old commodity but for something as basic as a vitally important foodstuff. Moreover, the companies are rather secretive about their operations.[1]

There are indeed good reasons for needing to know a little about the big grain traders, but there is precious little evidence that they operate in a way

1 There is extensive literature on these companies. See, for example, Dan Morgan, *Merchants of Grain*; Chapter 6 of Nick Butler's *The international grain trade;* J Trager, *The great grain robbery* and Richard Gilmore, *A poor harvest: The clash of policies and interests in the grain trade.*

that should make the public suspicious of them. The damage done to global welfare by misguided agricultural and trade policies is far greater than any threat posed by grain traders, not least because the policy makers who enact these policies claim to act in the general interest. Innovative and competitive companies making money from trading certainly do not cause the kind of misallocation of resources that is generated by the EC's Common Agricultural Policy, a fact their critics would do well to recognize.

The grain trading companies

There are five major international grain trading companies.[2] They are Cargill (whose European subsidiary is called Tradax), Continental Grain, Louis Dreyfus, Andre (also known as Garnac because of its US affiliate of that name) and Bunge and Born. Together, they probably account for three-quarters of the grain shipped internationally. The exact figure is not known and their share certainly varies from exporter to exporter and from grain to grain.[3] But no-one disputes the fact that they occupy an extremely large share of the world's grain trade.

What this means, in practice, is that these companies manage the physical flow of grain from the farm to the consumer. This can be seen with the aid of a simple example. Imagine that a Turkish feed manufacturer wants to buy sorghum for inclusion in premixed animal feeds and for wholesaling on to smaller manufacturers. He will contact the local office of one of the grain companies and outline the requirements in terms of quantity, quality, delivery point and delivery period. The company will respond with a price. The job of the company is then to move the grain to the delivery point and make a profit in doing so. This exposes the company to a large number of risks (or a large number of opportunities for profit, depending on one's perspective).

2 Readers will recall that the book's focus is on wheat and coarse grains. The grain trading companies are not so constrained: they actively trade soybeans, as well as a range of other agricultural (and, increasingly, non-agricultural) commodities. In this chapter, therefore, we shall use the word 'grain' rather more loosely than in the rest of the book.

3 In Canada and Australia, for example, wheat trade is controlled by government Wheat Boards. These organizations were established because of a feeling that their national interests would not be served by leaving wheat exports in private hands. Both the Australian and the Canadian Boards, however, can and do employ the major private grain companies to execute sales.

The company initially commits itself to a delivery price, based on its assessment of market conditions: this assessment will include not only the grain market, but the state of the shipping market and the foreign exchange market. Typically, customers in countries like Turkey, who trade more with Europe than with the US, are happier dealing in European currencies. Hence the grain company may well provide a quotation in Swiss Francs or Deutsche Marks, but since it will have to buy the grain in dollars, it exposes itself to currency risk. There is also the possibility that the company may not want to or be able to sell US grain. If the sale is for Australian sorghum, then the grain will have to be bought in Australia for Australian dollars. Either way, there may well be a currency risk involved in the sale.

At the time the company makes an offer to the Turkish customer, it may or may not have enough grain already in its possession to meet the order: it probably will not have chartered the shipping to carry the grain and it probably will not have an open position in the foreign exchange market. Once the customer accepts the offer, however, the company has to make a decision about when it will cover its risks. It is rarely that the company will cover all of its exposure immediately. Usually, it will cover those aspects of the exposure that it is worried will move disadvantageously, whereas it will leave open those positions that it expects to improve. Thus if the company believes sorghum prices will fall, it is likely not to buy the sorghum it needs to meet the order quickly. Rather, it will wait and allow a little extra profit to be made. So it goes with every part of the transaction. The shipping part is particularly complex, because the co-ordination of shipping within the exporting country to the port and the arrangement of international shipping provide scope for profit and loss. Since most grain shipments are rather less than the amount that will fit into a modern, efficient grain vessel, the company will try, as far as possible, to ship different orders together.

The company's ability to cover the risks of adverse price movements in the product, shipping and foreign exchange markets is limited. In the case of sorghum, for example, there is no futures market, but even in cases where there is a futures market, there is considerable basis risk. That is, in the case of a wheat sale, it may be possible to cover the amount of the sale in the Chicago market. But the delivery locations of the Chicago contract may not correspond to the locations where the company will, first, actually buy the grain and, second, load it onto an export vessel. The difference in the price of grain between Chicago and New Orleans, the major grain export port, may be no more than a few cents a bushel, and in the long run the difference will be equal to the cost of transportation between the two, but in the short period of time that grain companies deal in, the price difference can move by enough to wipe out (or to multiply several fold) its profit margin on the entire transaction. Similarly, in the shipping and foreign exchange markets, to the extent that hedging opportunities exist they may not exactly match the exporter's requirements.[4] Even where they exist, the exporter can always choose whether and when to hedge, exposing himself to the possibility of profit or loss for the time his position remains unhedged.

The job of the grain companies is, therefore, conceptually simple but in practice extremely complex. Moreover, their margins on individual sales tend to be quite low: they typically sell grain for only a few more cents per bushel than they pay for it. They make their profits out of good market judgement, prudent risk management and sales volume.

To this extent, therefore, they are no different from any other trading companies, nor, to this extent, are they any different from the way grain companies have always been. The risks in trading grain have always been great, and the history of the trade is replete with examples of larger-than-life traders who made (and often lost) fortunes on the grain market. The closing years of the last century and the opening years of this were particularly colourful. These were the years when US grain production and exports were expanding rapidly to meet the growing European, and especially British, demand for grain. In the 1870s Isaac Friedlander successfully cornered the supply of ships needed to transport California's grain crop to Liverpool and made a fortune, only to go bankrupt in 1877 when he made an inaccurate estimate of the size of the crop and chartered more vessels than he could use. In 1917 James Norris ran a trading company that had several large orders from Germany. When the US declared war on Germany in April, these contracts were rendered void, leaving Norris with large stocks of grain he was free to sell on the market, at the inflated prices that the state of war had brought. In such ways trading companies have always made money and the current five large companies can all trace their roots to the time when fortunes were made and lost in this way. Indeed, some of them have had direct experience of these ups and downs: Louis Dreyfus, for example, had built up a large asset base in Odessa, a major Russian grain port, only to lose everything after the revolution of 1917.

The modern grain companies do differ, however, from companies that trade other commodities and from their historical counterparts in a number of respects. Their key skills are the same that have been required of traders since time immemorial, but the context in which they operate is rather different.

In the first place, trade in agricultural commodities differs from trade in other commodities in that agricultural commodities tend to be more volatile in price than other products and are more likely to be produced by a very large number of individual producers. This is a crucial difference from the oil market, for example: although there are several large and important

4 These basis problems are particularly severe for non-US exporters. See Bond & Thompson, *Basis and exchange rate risk in offshore futures trading.*

independent oil trading companies, many of the largest trading groups are units of the big oil producing and refining companies. In the case of grain, there are no Exxons: even the biggest farmers in the US or elsewhere are tiny in relation to the world market. But note that grain has been volatile in price for almost all of its history as a traded commodity, whereas oil has been volatile in price for only a few years in its history: and this short period of time has seen the emergence of independent traders. This suggests that independent operators can thrive where producers cannot. After all, producers have a fundamental position to defend, whereas independents can thrive whether prices are high or low. They only need to make a margin.

The second way in which the modern companies differ from their antecedents is their size. Indeed, it is this size that has been at the heart of the debate over their role. There are really two aspects to their size: one is the volume of grain transactions they handle, and the other is the range of their activities. This latter, their diversity, is somewhat separate, and will be discussed below. The volume of their transactions does strike the casual observer as strange: after all, if trading is really just a form of entrepreneurship, where are the advantages in size?

There are a number of reasons why one should not be surprised at the size of the big grain companies. Grain is, after all, traded extremely widely, and the informational networks needed to operate on a global scale are so expensive that a firm would need a large turnover to justify the cost. Indeed the economies of scale in information are usually cited as the biggest barrier to new entrants to this business. The big grain companics have agents in every significant grain producing, exporting and importing nation, monitoring the weather, crop conditions, economic trends and political developments as well as the mundane business of seeking and processing orders for grain. There are also economies of scale in grain storage and transportation: and this is a major argument in favour of the diversification that the firms have undertaken. Greater size also provides better access to credit, and in trading, working capital is of fundamental importance. The cheaper that capital can be obtained, the stronger the trading company is. Finally, and perhaps most importantly, size provides for risk diversification. Each individual trade that a grain company enacts has the potential for high levels of profit, but it can also produce a large loss. One way in which the risk of overall loss can be guarded against is by engaging in a large number of trades. A diversified portfolio of trades spreads the risk, and makes the risk of catastrophic loss much lower. The grain companies' ability to move soybeans to the USSR, wheat to Brazil and maize to the Philippines gives them a degree of comfort, since they will not suffer unduly if one of the deals turns into a loss maker. Even better, if one deal turns sour, a large company is more likely to have the capacity to take that grain, wherever it might be in the marketing chain, and use it for another customer's order.

A third key difference with the modern companies, an aspect of their size which was referred to above, is their diversity. This diversity has taken many forms. Although there are some instances of the companies buying agricultural land, their integration has more usually involved activities related to grain distribution and processing rather than production. Their first integrations were into grain storage facilities and shipping. Louis Dreyfus has embraced shipping more enthusiastically than the other companies, and Cargill probably owns more storage space than the others, but they have all followed essentially the same pattern. The initial focus on storage and transportation facilities simply reflects the economies of scale in these businesses of which the large companies are able to take advantage. Later, they spread to a wide range of activities.

Bunge and Born, which began life based in Antwerp, Belgium and later shifted its headquarters to Argentina (and most recently again to Brazil), built an impressive industrial empire in Argentina, starting with flour mills and later encompassing soybean processing, paints (for which the oils from linseed and flaxseed are raw materials), textiles, fruit and vegetable growing and processing, banking, timber, real estate and joint-venture chemical production with large European companies. It is hard to overstate the importance of Bunge and Born, or B y B as it is known in Argentina, to the Argentine economy. When two scions of one of the founding families, Jorge and Juan Born, were kidnapped in Buenos Aires in 1974 by radical guerrillas, they were chosen precisely because they were potent symbols of Argentina's wealthy business elite. They were eventually released after a ransom was paid, claimed by the guerrillas to have been $60 million: an unprecedented sum that gave an insight into the financial resources of the company. Although this event prompted the company to move its headquarters to Brazil, it remained influential in Argentine life. After the election of Carlos Menem to the Argentine presidency in 1989, his Minister of Economy came from Bunge and Born and the anti-inflation programme he introduced was known as the 'plan B y B'. The links between the company and the government were made all the clearer when, only a few weeks into the job, the Minister died, only to be replaced by another Bunge and Born functionary.

It is Cargill that is perhaps the most diversified of the grain companies. Its range of activities is remarkable. Apart from its core business of trading grain and oilseeds, it is an active trader of other agricultural and non-agricultural commodities, including sugar, cotton, molasses, copra, salt, ores, concentrates and metals. Beyond trading, it has extensive holdings in transportation and related services (for example stevedoring) and in commodity storage facilities. It is also a large commodity processor, with interests in soybean crushing, cotton ginning and corn wet milling (from which HFCS, a sugar substitute, is made). Still in agriculture, it has companies involved with seeds, feeds, fertilizers, farm equipment, cattle feeding, meat packing and poultry production. Beyond agriculture, it has interests in the production of speciality steels, in chemicals, in insurance, in leasing and in brokerage services. This list is not comprehensive; and of course Cargill's activities are constantly changing as the company grows.

This pattern of diversification is partly explicable in terms of risk management, but such an explanation only goes so far, and certainly does not help to explain the different patterns of diversification from one company to another. To explain this, it is important to bear in mind one other distinguishing feature of these five companies; they are all privately held. There was once a major grain trader that was a publicly listed corporation, but it went bankrupt in 1977. It is highly unusual to find all the leading companies in an industry to be privately held; the fact that these trading companies are requires some explanation.

From a historical perspective, this tight control is easy to understand. Obtaining and acting on information has always been central to trading: it is an information-intensive business. In the nineteenth century, when information flowed less easily than it does today, and when local agents had to be entrusted with considerable autonomy, there was a clear advantage in retaining trading companies as family concerns. The family tie could be relied upon to provide a bond of loyalty and trust. Hence the early trading companies grew up around families and are still controlled by family interests: Cargill by the MacMillans, Bunge and Born by the Born and Hirsch families and Continental by the Fribourgs. The families who gave their names to Andre and Louis Dreyfus still control those companies. Having established themselves as family companies, they have never seen a reason to go public and have not needed access to the public capital market: the fact that they are private means that it is not possible to get information on their profitability, but it must be the case that they are profitable enough to generate the funds needed for expansion. It may also be the case that, as privately controlled companies, they have been able to invest with a longer time horizon than publicly traded companies who have external stockholders to satisfy.[5]

Clearly, the big five grain trading companies are unusual, in addition to being large and diversified multinational companies. There are good economic

5 This is clearly a complicated subject, and one with a vast literature all of its own. It is important to note, however, that, within the grain companies, it appears as though control is very highly valued. Of course, this may be no more than a legacy of a time when loyalty was so important. It may reflect, however, the continuing value to the companies of keeping information secret for as long as possible. One should not dismiss too lightly the historical explanation: the families behind both Continental and Louis Dreyfus have direct personal experience of asset appropriation when they had to flee France ahead of the occupying German forces.

reasons for them to be large and diversified: their size and diversity allow them to exploit economies of scale in information gathering, storage and transportation and to diversify their risks. But is it a matter of public concern that these companies, who are so important to the distribution of so essential a commodity, are so large?

Does the companies' size matter?

The public would have a legitimate concern if one (or both) of two things were true. Have the companies ever acted against the public interest in a way that could not or cannot be redressed using ordinary legal means? Secondly, do the companies act in an anti-competitive manner?

There is of course a great deal of activity in any economy that is best characterized as a cat and mouse game between economic agents and the regulatory/legal authorities. Accountants are employed to find and exploit tax loopholes: the tax authorities close loopholes, only to find that developments in the world of clever accountants open up new ones. Certainly, the grain market has seen its fair share of this kind of activity. One particularly sensitive area has been technical standards for grain. Under standard international grain trade contracts, there are clauses specifying the moisture level of the grain, the percentage of non-grain matter and so on. It is clearly in a trader's interest not to exceed the minimum quality levels specified in the contract. There have been numerous cases in the past of extremely sharp practice and there have also been cases of senior executives from certain companies being convicted of violating standards and even being imprisoned. It was a long time complaint of Soviet grain purchasers that US shipments of grain were consistently of a lower quality than those of other exporters. The concern that repeated scandals were harming the market reputation of the US led to a legal remedy; the establishment of a federal grain inspection service charged with regulating the quality of grain and classifying it according to accepted quality standards.

It is hard to imagine that this kind of abuse owes anything to the structure of the grain trading industry. Indeed, the fact that companies feel under pressure to boost their margins by this kind of practice may be a sign of the extreme competitiveness of the market. Certainly, the grain market is not alone in having to deal with such abuses; it would probably be hard to think of an industry that did not have similar problems. One may complain that the regulatory authorities are slow in responding to problems, that they lack teeth, that they are too lenient or that they are too close to the people they are supposed to be regulating; but these complaints, however legitimate they may be, are certainly not unique to the grain market.

Similarly, complaints that the grain traders have excessive political influence are also misplaced. Again, it is true that, like other US corporations, they are well represented in Washington, but, if they are successful as lobbyists, their success is no more than a reflection of the general strength of the agricultural lobby. To the extent that they seek policies that encourage agricultural exports (since volume is good for their business), they are merely part of a broad coalition of agricultural interests. Certainly, the grain companies have been unsuccessful in many individual issues on which they have chosen to take a strong position: they argued forcefully against the US grain embargo of the Soviet Union, for example, and they have also often opposed various features of US farm policy.

A key test for economists of the grain companies' power would be their ability to affect prices. On this, there are three separate points to be made. In the first place, to the extent that traders make their profits out of their margins, they do not really care what the absolute level of prices is. They can make money whether prices are high or low, rising, falling or stable. Over the longer term they have no interest in affecting the level of prices. In the second place, however, it is in their interest to try to influence prices in the short run. For example, a company that has just received a large export order has every incentive to conceal the order until it has made its purchases. To the extent that the margin between its buying and selling prices can be influenced, the company's profit margins can be increased. It does seem likely that the companies are large enough to have a short term influence on the market: there are frequent stories circulating in the market about big companies trying to affect the closing price in Europe or in Chicago in order to improve their margins. These stories are commonly believed by traders, and although there is no concrete evidence of price manipulation, it does seem likely that it does occur. It should also be remembered that, in a low-margin business like trading, a tiny variation in prices can make a large difference to profit levels. Moreover, the variation in prices over the course of a day or a week would make it hard to tell whether high profits and a particular transaction was the result of price manipulation or simply good market judgement.

Thirdly, however, and most importantly, it is quite widely recognized that, in the long term, grain prices are determined by the forces of supply and demand: a mixture of agricultural policy, the weather, technology, population trends, macroeconomic performance and other economic factors. This set of influences is far too powerful to allow much room for trading companies. They do not have the kind of influence over prices that should be of concern to the general public. The general public ought to be far more concerned over the impact of agricultural policies enacted by policy makers supposedly acting in the public interest.

The economist's concern with whether trading companies can affect prices is one way of asking whether the grain market is competitive, or rather whether the grain companies compete. Certainly, they do compete, often fiercely, for business: there is nothing like the cosy cartel that can be found in the world chemical business, for example. One way of considering this is by looking at the existence and nature of barriers to new entrants into the business.

There is a formidable barrier of entry into the grain trading business. It arises because of the economies of scale in transportation, distribution and information gathering. These make it very difficult for an entrepreneur to begin trading grain on a scale likely to trouble the big players. Of course, there are many grain trading companies, most of which are small. The days are far from over when a clever trader could make a fortune from a few well-timed deals. These barriers to entry are not insurmountable, however, as two developments show.

One is the story of Cook Industries, a trading company run by a remarkable entrepreneur, Ned Cook. His father had built up a cotton trading business in the southern US and this trading experience was used by the son as a basis for expansion into soybean and grain trading. To finance this expansion (in particular to finance the acquisition of grain storage facilities near the mouth of the Mississippi) Cook took his company public, giving analysts a rare insight into the finances of grain trading companies.[6] Cook was, initially, extremely successful: he was able to take advantage of the changed dynamics of the grain markets in the early 1970s, and particularly the opening up of the Soviet market, to build a grain trading company big enough to rival the established firms.

Cook's firm collapsed, however, in 1978, largely the result of a huge gamble on the soybean market. Cook Industries had developed a reputation for aggressive, speculative transactions, designed to supplement the more modest profits made on physical shipments of grain. Having developed a view that soybean prices would decline, Cook began to sell the market short, building up an ever larger position. Unfortunately for Cook, soybean prices did not behave in the way the firm had expected, and the resultant losses were so large (in excess of $80 million) that they forced the firm into a major retrenchment. It lost its status as one of the biggest grain trading firms.

This story illustrates that entry into the business is possible; it also illustrates that careful risk management is an essential tool that needs to be employed continuously in trading. When an unhedged position is allowed

6 In the early days, people marvelled at how profitable the business was. Cook Industries' pre-tax profits rose from $4 mn in 1972 to $40 mn in 1973, largely due to the Russian grain sales.

to expand, losses can mount to the point where they threaten a company's survival. (A convincing demonstration that companies have little influence on the behaviour of prices.)

The Cook episode laid the groundwork for what may prove, over the long run, to be a more significant development. The purchaser of one of Cook Industries' major assets, a large elevator on the Mississippi, was Mitsui, the giant Japanese trading firm. This marked the beginning of a slow but steady move by the Japanese into the US grain market. By the early 1990s, Zen-Noh (a large agricultural co-operative), Mitsui and Marubeni all owned grain storage and handling facilities in several areas of the US. When these investments began, it appeared as though they were simply part of a strategy to guarantee access to supplies in the US that could be used for shipment to Japan, a trade route on which companies earn handsome profits (thanks to the Japanese government's regulations governing grain imports). More recently, however, it appears that the Japanese companies are beginning to seek out profitable deals involving third parties: in 1990 they made some sales of US grain to the Soviet Union. Obviously, these Japanese trading companies have the financial capacity, the global information network and the risk management skills to pose a major competitive threat to the established companies.

Similarly, the Italian company, Ferruzzi, expanded its agricultural trading activities rapidly during the 1980s. It is an extremely widely diversified corporation and is increasingly active in US grain markets. Like the Japanese trading companies, it has the global network and the financial strength to constitute a serious competitive challenge to the established major grain companies.

Grain trading companies – some conclusions

There is a school of thought that holds that, since the grain companies are so large and have so large a role in the distribution of so important a commodity, there must be legitimate public concern about their activities. In fact, they are competitive: they exert no significant influence on prices even though they may be able to affect short term movements in some markets; they face the threat of entry into their business by Japanese competitors, and there can be absolutely no doubt that any market distortions they cause are insignificant compared to the distortions engendered by agricultural policy makers. Naturally, their activities need to be overseen by the appropriate authorities, and there will always be room for improvement in corporate and regulator behaviour. But concern over the grain companies seems somewhat misplaced.

CHAPTER

10

Grain futures markets

The emergence and workings of futures markets

Futures markets play a vitally important role in the world's grain trade. They are also increasingly of interest to private investors, attracted by the excitement of futures trading and the (remote) chance of large profits. Many people have seen futures exchanges on television, and the image they present, of throngs of young people screaming and gesticulating at each other, is not one that suggests these markets play a role that is of interest and concern to the broader public. How did they emerge, how do they work, and what exactly is the role played by these institutions?

Futures markets grew out of forward markets. A forward market is like a spot, or cash, market, in that it establishes a contractual obligation between two parties to buy and sell a specified good at an agreed price. In a spot market, delivery is immediate, whereas in a forward market delivery is at a predetermined point in the future. Forward markets have existed for a very long time, but they became popular instruments when world agricultural trade began to expand in the eighteenth century. The reason they grew was price volatility. In the absence of forward markets, merchants take great risks; they gamble that the goods they bought three months ago in a far away location can be sold here and now at a price high enough to cover the costs of the transaction and provide a profit. If prices fall in the meantime, the merchant will take a heavy loss on his inventory. The more volatile prices are, the greater the risks of engaging in this business. Users face similar problems. A flour miller needs a steady input of wheat to allow production of flour year round. The miller could buy a year's worth of stocks at harvest time, but then he would face the high costs of storing the grain. Relying on the spot market exposes him to the risk that the price of his input will vary from one month to the next, possibly putting him at a competitive disadvantage to other millers.

When prices are volatile, therefore, there are many market participants whose risks are high and who have a powerful incentive to try to establish, with a reasonable degree of certainty, what prices will be in the future.

Hence the origin of forward markets. Imagine a forward contract between a wheat merchant and a flour miller. With this contract, calling, say, for the miller's annual requirements to be delivered in four instalments, the miller knows fairly precisely what her key input cost will be for the season; so she will be able to offer forward contracts to her customers. She will also be able to save on her working capital needs, since she can keep her stock levels lower. The merchant reduces his risk of inventory loss while shipping grain.

Forward markets did not remove all sources of risk, however. Notably, they did not remove the risk of counterparty default. In a spot market, there is no risk of counterparty default, because the entire transaction is completed at one time.[1] In a forward market, the risk of counterparty default is quite high and such a default can be costly. Go back to the case of the miller above, who has used her forward contract with the wheat merchant to enter into forward contracts with her customers. What if the merchant goes out of business and the miller has to cover her needs on the spot market where, let us imagine, the price of wheat has gone up? The problem is that forward contracts, being specific to two parties, do not have an active secondary market. A different miller, with needs for a different quality of grain delivered at different times of the year, would only buy the first miller's contract at a large discount.

Futures markets grew up as a solution to these problems.[2] People wanted to have a mechanism whereby forward prices could be established, to reduce the risks of doing business with volatile spot markets. But they also needed a system with greater flexibility and lower risk than specific forward

1 Of course, there may be a counterparty risk if the seller offers the buyer credit to pay for the purchase. But credit risk is a whole new ball game that we shall not discuss here.

2 They emerged in North America and Europe in the second half of the nineteenth century, but there is evidence that a rice futures market existed in Japan in the eighteenth century. For more details, see Atkin, *Agricultural commodity markets*.

contracts. A futures contract, therefore, has two important features that differentiate it from a forward market. In the first place, futures contracts are standardized with respect to quality factors, delivery locations, dispute procedures and so on. Only price is free to move. This means that all other, local, buyer and seller specific factors, such as one miller's need for high protein wheat and another's for low protein wheat, are abstracted from, allowing the market to concentrate on the price alone.[3] Secondly, the futures market gets around counterparty risk through an institution called a clearing house.

A futures market (such as the Chicago Board of Trade) consists essentially of a place where traders meet to trade standardized contracts for goods. A futures trading 'pit', or 'floor' is the place where all the screaming and gesticulating goes on. Once two traders have agreed to exchange a contract, that single contract, with one buyer and one seller, is registered with the clearing house and transformed into two contracts, each with the clearing house as the counterparty. Thus the seller, who agreed on the floor to sell to the other trader, now agrees to sell to the clearing house, and the buyer agrees to buy from the clearing house. Note that everyone's net position is the same; the seller has an obligation to sell (at the determined price), the buyer has an obligation to buy and the clearing house, with an obligation to buy and one to sell (both at the same price) has no net obligation.

This greatly facilitates trading. If the original seller wishes to close out his obligation to sell, he does not have to track down the original buyer and agree to tear up the original contract. He can simply reach a new agreement with a new trader under which he will buy. This new trade gets transformed by the clearing house, and our original seller now has two obligations; his original one to sell to the clearing house, and his new obligation to buy from the clearing house. His net position is simply any difference in price between these two contracts, which he takes either as a profit or as a loss (depending on how prices have moved). Again, since the counterparty to each trade is the clearing house, the clearing house makes neither profit nor loss; it simply takes in losses from some and pays out profits to others.

It is a consequence of this that is sometimes confusing to those who are new to futures trading, that there is no finite stock of contracts that can be exchanged. The terms of any contract are standardized, but any willing buyer and willing seller can agree to buy or sell, thereby creating a contract. And the obligations created by this contract can be closed out by taking an

3 This means that certain risks remain; for example the risk that the price difference between the standard grade quoted on the futures market and the grade a particular purchaser wants will vary. The difference between the futures market price and the price for a particular grade in a particular location is called the basis. And the residual risk is called the basis risk.

opposite position in a new contract, leaving only the financial difference to be settled by the clearing house.[4] Because of the ease of taking out offsetting contracts, there is very little use of futures markets as a physical delivery mechanism. Traders can deliver physical commodities as their contracts expire, and they can take delivery, but well over 90% of futures transactions are closed out by offsetting futures positions, once the risk of dealing in the cash market has been dealt with.

The advantages of this system are obvious. Of course, no trading system can entirely remove the risk inherent in a market where prices are volatile, but the risks can be passed on to those most willing to bear them. An important feature of futures contracts is that they create a symmetrical set of rights and obligations. Imagine the position of a speculative buyer of wheat, who buys on the futures market in the expectation that prices will rise, allowing him to make a profit. If prices rise, his original contract gives him the right to buy at the lower price specified in his contract. So if he sells at the higher price, he will make a profit. But this right to buy is also an obligation to buy; if prices fall, he has no choice but to take a loss.

Options are contracts that do not create symmetrical rights and obligations. Although options have been around for a very long period of time, they were not allowed to be formally traded on US commodity exchanges until 1983. Briefly, options work in the following way.[5] An option to buy (a call option) creates a right to buy at a specified price, but the holder need not exercise the right if he chooses not to. An option to sell (a put option) creates the right to sell, but again it need not be exercised. Clearly, the person who grants, or writes, the option faces a much higher risk than the person who holds the option. Consider the grantor of a call option, who gives someone the right to buy 5,000 bushels of wheat in three months time at $3.50 per bushel. If the three months pass, and the price of wheat is $3.00, the option is worthless and it will simply expire. But if the price of wheat rises to $5.00, the option will be worth a lot of money: $1.50 per bushel, or $7,500 for the 5,000 bushel contract. The option grantor will demand some compensation for the extra risk he is carrying; hence he will

4 Readers looking for a more thorough treatment of the mechanics of trading should consult a more specialized text, such as the present author's *Agricultural commodity markets*, or one of its many competitors. It is worth pointing out that floor traders on futures markets are limited in number. They may be independent traders, or they may work for large trading or financial services companies. 'Commission houses' are firms that provide trading services in return for commissions. A very large number of brokerages provide access to the markets for outside users.

5 This is a rather complicated subject, and interested readers will need to follow the subject up elsewhere. A good start can be made with Chapter 2 of Atkin, *Agricultural commodity markets*.

charge a price for the option. The price will be a function of the risk, that is, how likely he thinks it will be that he will make a loss.

The role of futures markets in grain

The above discussion made it clear that a primary function of futures markets is to allow market participants to manage the risks they face. In fact, there are some other important functions, and there is a little more to say about this risk management role.

Hedging and the price of storage

Chapter 9 illustrated how an important function of a grain marketing system is to accommodate the seasonal pattern of production. The provision of adequate storage facilities is a key component of this. In normal circumstances, the market must provide a return to the providers of storage. Early economic analysis of futures markets suggested that the price (quoted today) of a good at some point in the future should approximate the price of the good today plus the costs of storing it from today until the relevant point in the future. Research confirms that, in normal conditions, the structure of futures prices corresponds to the costs of storage. The difference between the spot and the futures price is called a 'carrying charge' or a 'carry' in the US, whereas in the UK it is known as a 'contango'. The price of storage (i.e. the contango) is, of course, itself an economic price, set by supply and demand. If the market expects a shortage of grain at some point in the future, there should be encouragement to forego current consumption and, instead, store the grain for future use. This will result in a high price for storage. Conversely, if abundance is expected in the future, the market will not reward storage. Consider the example of a bad harvest, which leaves tight supply conditions. As spring comes around, imagine that conditions are good and there is every reason to expect the next harvest to be good. Under these circumstances, the market would convey incentives not to store grain; the upcoming harvest will look after future needs, and grain is needed now to compensate for last season's poor harvest. Hence the incentive to store will be removed, and the futures price will fall below the cash price. This relationship is known as a backwardation in the UK, but, again, the American term, 'inverse carrying charge', conveys the economic significance.

The relationship between the structure of futures prices and the costs of storing grain allows people who provide storage facilities to use the markets actively, hedging their risks.

At this point, it is useful to say what futures prices are not. They are not necessarily to be seen as forecasts of spot prices in the future. That is, in January one can find a quotation for March delivery wheat. By the time March comes along, the cash price may or may not be what the March futures price was in January. In providing a price for March wheat, the market is not providing a forecast of what it thinks the cash price will be in March. With a storable commodity such as grain, the existence of stocks provides a link between futures and cash prices that does not exist for all goods. If it were not possible to store a product, then the futures price would represent expectations of supply and demand for that future period. For example, there is a futures contract for live cattle. These are slaughter ready beasts, and clearly they cannot be stored; their age, weight and meat quality would all change if they were 'stored'. In such a case, a futures price represents the market expectation of supplies and demands at the time specified in the futures contract. Thus a bad winter storm that killed a large number of young cattle would affect expected supplies for the interval during which these animals would be coming to market. Prices for that period would be affected. Other prices would only be affected to the extent that farmers could adjust their feeding schedules to smooth out the supply disruption.

With grain, the position is different, because there is no price-affecting information that is relevant only to the future. Poor weather during the growing season will affect the prices of new crop grain; but the price of the old crop will also be affected because the market will need to ration existing supplies to cover the expected future shortfall. Hence spot prices will go up. It is certainly the case that spot prices contain an expectational element; clearly, the price of grain now is affected by what the market expects supply and demand to be in the future. In so far as spot prices reflect expectations, futures prices do. But there is little independent expectational element in the futures price of a storable good.

Price discovery and liquidity

Another important function of the futures market is to provide a public source of prices. The Chicago Board of Trade, the world's most important futures exchange, started life as a meeting place where merchants would make open deals for grain, to overcome widespread suspicion that honest dealers were being shortchanged by the lack of clear public sources of prices. The prices set on the floor of a futures exchange are logged into a computer, transmitted by electronic news services immediately and published in newspapers. Hence everyone can easily find out what the price is, and the price can serve as a marker for deals done away from the exchange.

It is clearly desirable that this futures price, if it is to be useful for the physical trade, should reflect a good volume of buying and selling; i.e. the market should be liquid. The ease of trading futures (compared with trading physical grain, for example) helps to ensure this liquidity. Both buyers and sellers like to feel that they can transact their business without having an effect on the price, and this is only so if the market is liquid. By standardizing all the details of grain quality, delivery terms etc, the futures market maximizes liquidity. Without liquidity, markets fail because the prices they set are not accepted as fair and accurate prices.

The provision of credit

Futures markets help in the provision of credit to the agricultural marketing chain. An inventory that is hedged has a known value, and can be offered as collateral for a loan. Unhedged, the value of an inventory can fluctuate dramatically and its value as collateral is therefore less.

Reducing uncertainty and volatility

A final important role of futures markets is to reduce uncertainty and volatility. Price volatility in itself is not necessarily a bad thing, because a price change is a signal to economic actors to change their behaviour. But unexpected price changes (i.e. uncertainty) do cause efficiency losses, because they make production, marketing and consumption decisions much more difficult. Futures markets allow hedging to take place and for this reason reduce the uncertainty that is associated with volatility. Moreover, active futures trading tends to reduce the extent of underlying volatility in prices. The increased market liquidity that futures trading provides tends to cause prices to be less volatile than they are in less liquid markets.[6]

6 This is perhaps a controversial statement. Certainly there is evidence that all markets are prone to speculative excesses, and economic history is replete with examples, from London's eighteenth century South Sea Bubble, to Tokyo's real estate market in the 1980s. The 1974 bull market in sugar is widely held to be another example, and I certainly do not wish to claim that futures markets are exempt from such speculative excesses. The evidence is very strong, however, in markets as diverse as cotton, wheat, onions, live cattle and pork bellies, that futures markets tend to stabilize cash market prices. For the relevant evidence, see Atkin, *Agricultural commodity markets*, especially footnote 8 to Chapter 1.

The use of futures and options markets by hedgers and speculators

The mechanics of futures trading are really very simple: all one needs is an account with a commission house. The costs of transactions are low (that is to say, the commissions charged are normally low), but there is a need to post a good faith deposit, called an initial margin, which is deposited with the clearing house. This initial margin is, again, usually small; it is set by the exchange and can vary, and is lower for hedgers than for speculators, but is rarely more than 10% of the nominal value of the total contract. For example, the Chicago Board of Trade (CBOT) wheat contract is a 5,000 bushel contract, quoted in dollars per bushel. Say the wheat price is \$3.50 per bushel. The nominal value of a 5,000 bushel contract therefore is \$17,500. The amount of money needed to control this contract would normally be less than \$2,000. If the price of wheat varies (and thus the value of the contract varies) the exchange will demand (or credit) additional funds, called variation margin. If the value of the trader's contract has gone up, the exchange credits funds to his account. If the value has gone down, funds are demanded to remove the incentive for default. The important point is that it does not cost very much to trade on the markets, which makes them attractive to both hedgers and speculators. For hedgers, it means a large inventory can be hedged at very low cost. For speculators it means the potential for large profits for a small outlay.

Consider the example above of wheat at \$3.50 per bushel, and imagine that a speculator, who thinks wheat prices will rise, takes out a contract to buy at this price, making an outlay of \$2,000. Imagine that wheat prices go up by 25 cents. At \$3.75 per bushel, a 5,000 bushel contract is worth \$18,750, up \$1,250 and representing a profit to the speculator. (Of course, when he closes out his trade, he gets his initial margin money back.) Speculators like futures markets for three main reasons. Firstly, because the initial outlays are small, they provide the opportunity for highly leveraged activity. Secondly, since the prices of futures are volatile (without price volatility there would exist no incentive to have a futures market) they provide the possibility of large profits. Thirdly, it is as easy to profit from price declines as from price rises, since short selling in futures is as easy as buying. Speculators are a very heterogeneous bunch, ranging from professional traders in the pits who put huge sums to work in the markets to ordinary citizens who enjoy an occasional flutter; they are united only in their willingness to carry risk and their eagerness to make a profit.

Taking out a simple long or short position, known as a straight position, is only one of a range of speculative trading opportunities available, however. There are a number of possibilities to trade spreads, whereby one takes a view not on an absolute price change but on a relative price change. Take the example of the wheat-maize spread, which is very commonly traded. Chapter 7 outlined that the price relationship between wheat and maize is variable. Imagine that wheat is $3.00 per bushel and maize is $2.20, and that a speculator thinks this difference will widen from 80 cents to $1.10. But he does not know whether maize prices will fall, wheat prices will rise, both will fall but maize by more, both will rise but wheat by more, or some other combination. The proper vehicle for such a trading view is a spread, long of wheat and short of maize. Table 10.1 shows the outcome of this trade with different possible prices of wheat and maize, based on the assumption that the speculator is right. Both the wheat and maize contracts on the CBOT are 5,000 bushel contracts.

Table 10.1 Outcome of trade using varying wheat/maize prices

	Wheat, $	**Maize, $**
Initial price	3.00	2.20
Contract value	15,000	11,000
Ending price 1	3.10	2.00
Contract value	15,500	10,000
Profit/loss	500	1,000
Ending price 2	3.70	2.60
Contract value	18,500	13,000
Profit/loss	3,500	−2,000
Ending price 3	2.95	1.85
Contract value	14,750	9,250
Profit/loss	−250	1,750

Obviously, it would be possible to give more examples, but the point should be clear; a spread trade allows one to take a view (and profit from it, if correct) on a price ratio. The total overall profit may come from a combination of profits and losses on the component trades; but the spread trader does not really care about absolute price changes. Spread trades generally (but not always) are less risky, than straight trades, but to the extent they are less risky they have a lesser profit potential.

There are a number of other kinds of spread trades that are commonly used in the grain markets. There are delivery spreads, where different months are traded against each other. This is commonly done in the form of a new crop/old crop spread, whereby traders attempt to take advantage of information that affects one crop more than another. In the wheat market, there is also the protein spread. There are futures contracts on the CBOT and on the Kansas City and Minneapolis exchanges, each for a different kind of wheat. (Chicago's is soft red winter; hard red winter is traded in Kansas City and hard spring wheat in Minneapolis.) These markets can be traded against each other, to take advantage of expected movements in the protein premium. Given the different growing cycles of winter and spring wheats, changes in weather conditions can affect the wheat market in ways that give speculators opportunities for profit.

Hedgers, on the other hand, though a heterogeneous group, are, like speculators, united in their attitude to risk. But whereas speculators embrace risk in the search for profit, hedgers are risk-averse. How hedgers use futures markets to reduce (but not to eliminate) risk can be seen with a small number of simple examples.

Consider first the farmer. The futures market allows him to sell his crop forward, thereby locking in a price ahead of harvest. Imagine a maize farmer is expecting a 60,000 bushel crop and that the current price for new crop futures is $2.50 per bushel. At this price, the farmer can make a decent profit, but he is worried that prices will fall over the months before he can bring in his harvest. So he can sell 12 contracts on the CBOT at $2.50. If prices do decline, to, say, $2.00/bushel, the price he will realize from the sale of his maize in the cash market will be $120,000 (i.e. 60,000 bushels at $2.00/bushel). But his short futures position will be profitable: since he has 'sold' 12 contracts at $2.50, he can buy them back on the futures market for $2.00/bushel, yielding a profit of 50 cents/bushel, or $30,000. His total revenue, therefore, is $150,000: the same as if he had sold his crop at a cash price of $2.50/bushel. (Obviously he would have incurred some trading costs, which we are ignoring.)

Note two important features of this farmer hedge. The first is that we have abstracted from the problem of production uncertainty. The farmer cannot know in advance exactly what his crop will be. In short selling 60,000 bushels, he runs the risk that, if his crop is less than 60,000 bushels, he will make less of a profit on the deal. This is an important reason why few farmers use futures markets directly, and when they do, they only hedge part of their crop.[7] But it is an illustration of the important fact that there is no such thing as a perfect hedge.

The second is this. What happens if the farmer is wrong about prices, and they rise, to $3.00 per bushel? His harvest is worth a lot more: $180,000. But his futures position under these circumstances would be showing a loss of 50 cents/bushel, or $30,000. So his net position is a revenue of $150,000. In hedging, the farmer has denied himself the possibility of increased profits.

As another kind of hedging, consider a grain elevator that buys 100,000

7 It appears to be the case that farmers prefer using forward contracts; see Nelson *Forward and futures contracts . . .* and Paul et al, *Farmers' use of forward contracts and futures*. Even though they may not use futures contracts much, farmers benefit from their presence because of the greater efficiency they bring to the marketing chain.

bushels of wheat from farmers, but does not have a specific customer for the grain. The price paid will reflect developments in the futures markets; let us say it was five cents under the nearest contract month in Chicago. The elevator now holds an inventory and is exposed to the risk of loss if prices decline. What is more, the costs of storing the grain have to be met. The solution is to sell 100,000 bushels forward on the futures market. As a result of this transaction, the elevator achieves two goals. Any fall (rise) in the value of the inventory will be offset by a rise (fall) in the value of the futures contract. Also, the elevator 'earns the carry', because the futures price, at which the grain was sold, will be higher than the cash price at which the grain was bought by the amount of the carrying charge. As in the case of the farmer hedge, this is not a perfect hedge, because the basis could alter; and again the possibility of windfall profits is eliminated.

As a third example, consider a grain exporting company that has been invited to tender for a country's wheat imports. The company does not know whether or not it will gain the business so it does not want to buy physical grain. Instead, it buys futures and uses this price to determine its tender. With the price determined, it can acquire the physical grain (and lift the hedge) whenever it wishes to. Or conversely, it may buy grain from farmers without a specific customer in mind, even though it knows there will be export demand in the months ahead. In this case, it is in the same position as the elevator operator in the previous example. The big grain companies choose very carefully whether to hedge or not to hedge; if they are confident that prices will move in one direction or another, they may leave a cash market position unhedged, to benefit from the increased profits the changes bring about.

The exporting example casts some interesting light on the process of tendering, which is an important part of the marketing chain, see Chapter 8. It is by far the most common way in which developing countries buy grain, yet it is rather inefficient because it imposes uncertainty on those invited to tender and they will demand compensation for this uncertainty. An alternative method would be for a developing country to buy futures, and then hold a tender for the shipping and delivery services. The futures contracts could simply be transferred to the lowest bidder; indeed, the tender could be set up so that discounts or premiums to the futures price would be quoted.

It is something of a mystery why such a system is not more commonly used. In part it reflects a lack of understanding about how futures markets work, and in part it reflects preference for existing, well established trade channels that allow scope for corruption. There are reasons to expect that this will change, see Chapter 11.

Options open up a different set of possibilities for both hedgers and speculators. Consider the farmer who wishes to hedge his 60,000 bushel maize crop. There are two options strategies that are used by some farmers to improve their positions. One is to buy put options. As in the above example, imagine that maize prices are $2.50/bushel and the farmer thinks this is a good price. Instead of selling futures, however, imagine that he buys 12 put options with a strike price of $2.50, and that for these he has to pay ten cents each.[8] (This is called the premium, not the price, to differentiate it clearly from the strike price.) If cash market prices fall to $2.00, his crop will sell for $120,000, but his put options will be worth 50 cents (the difference between the strike price and the cash price). However, he had to pay ten cents for these options, so his average realized return is $2.40/bushel, or $144,000. This is inferior to the futures hedging strategy, but what happens when prices rise? Imagine the price at harvest is $3.00/bushel. In this case, the farmer will sell his crop on the cash market for a return of $180,000, and he will simply abandon the options. His total return, therefore, is $2.90/bushel: the $3.00 cash price minus the ten cent premium paid for the options that have been abandoned. This is clearly superior to the futures strategy.

A second possibility is to write, or grant call options. These give the option purchaser the right to buy from the farmer, at harvest time, a futures contract for the strike price. Consider the farmer writes 12 call options at a strike price of $2.50/bushel, for which he receives a premium of ten cents. If prices fall to $2.00, the options will be abandoned, and the farmer sells his crop on the cash market for $2.00. However he receives the extra ten cents from the option premium and realizes a return of $2.10. If prices rise to $3.00, the farmer receives $180,000 from the cash market, but his option position is showing a loss; the options are now worth 50 cents, and he received only ten cents for them. His total return, therefore, will be $2.60/bushel.

The variety of option trades commonly used in the grain market by hedgers and speculators is remarkable. They go by such names as bull call spreads, bear call spreads, bull put spreads, bear put spreads and straddles. Options can be 'naked' or 'covered' and spreads can be 'vertical' or 'horizontal'. The important point about them is that they have different risk/reward characteristics than futures, and they therefore allow trades to be constructed that reflect the preferences of the traders, be they hedgers or speculators, and their assessments of future price directions.

8 In putting the premium at this level we are abstracting from the problem of what actually determined option prices. But this is such a complex subject it cannot be addressed satisfactorily in this context.

Techniques of price forecasting

An assessment of likely price movements is a central component of decision making by both hedgers and speculators. Speculators will only take up a trading position if they have a view of what prices are likely to do; and although hedgers are risk averse, it is the case that they frequently will decide not to hedge a position, or to hedge only part of the position, if they have a strong view of the likely course of prices. A large part of trading and judging prices is experience and the kind of understanding of markets that comes with experience. This is particularly important when balancing risks and rewards and deciding the precise timing of entering and exiting a trade.

Apart from intuition, there are two main approaches to price forecasting, the fundamental and the technical. Again, these are subjects about which entire books have been written, but the important features of both approaches can be presented.

Fundamental analysis

Fundamental analysis relates price movements to changes in supply and demand conditions; it is, therefore, the kind of price analysis with which economists are most comfortable. In one sense, fundamental analysis is 'correct', in that no-one doubts that changes in supplies and demands do determine price movements. A drought in the Great Plains will push up wheat prices because it reduces available supplies. Demand tends not to change in quite as dramatic a way, but, over the longer term, the growth in incomes in major consumers has had an effect on grain prices, and especially on coarse grain prices.

One needs to go a little beyond simple concepts of supply and demand for price analysis, however. There are a number of features of grain markets that one needs to pay attention to. Seasonality is obviously very important. The fact that world production surges in the months when the northern hemisphere harvests its grain does not lead to a sudden fall in prices. Grain consumption by livestock is higher in the winter months when pasture is not available. To the extent that these seasonal patterns conform to market expectations, there will be no price response.

Stocks are also extremely important. As discussed in Chapter 7, the stock/consumption ratio is a useful tool in understanding price movements, but the absolute level of stocks is not what is important. Seasonality is important, as is who controls the stocks. Private stock holders do not have the same reasons for holding stocks as the government. To the extent that the government holds stocks under clearly announced rules, each bushel of grain held in government stocks has different implications for prices than a bushel held by private stock holders.

Thirdly, one needs to be sensitive to policy. Agricultural policy decisions made in Brussels or Washington can have a pronounced effect on prices, in both the longer term and the shorter term. Over the longer term, for example, there can be no doubt that generous EC price supports in the 1980s led to increased production that, when exported, depressed world market prices. In the short term, the export subsidy programmes run by the EC and the US affect prices; particular deals done can move short term prices by several cents per bushel.

The difficulty with fundamental analysis is translating the general principle that supply and demand determine prices into working assessments of by how much prices will move in response to any given change in supply and demand fundamentals. Statistical techniques are used to quantify the impact of these changes, but they tend to work better when used to analyze the longer term movements of prices. Indeed, for long term price forecasting, there really is no alternative to these statistical methods. For short term analysis, however, they do not work as well; it is very hard to build a model that is sensitive to the daily flow of information into the markets, and as prices move up and down by a few cents in response to these changes, the trader whose position is based on a longer term view of fundamentals can lose a lot of money. Part of the problem here is the role of expectations. In longer term analysis, there are a number of techniques that can be used to incorporate expectations, but in the short term, expectations change so quickly and not always for obvious reasons, that it is very difficult to build a statistical model nimble enough to incorporate them.

Nonetheless, econometric models are quite widely used in the grain markets, not for day-to-day trading decisions, but to provide background analysis of the likely movements in prices over a period of several months. Few people trade solely on the basis of fundamentals, and many people ignore them, especially traders with short time horizons.

Technical analysis

Technical analysis is more commonly used for short term trades, and it is also widely used to complement an assessment of fundamentals. Even though technical analysis is commonly used, its intellectual foundation is not very convincing, and few people who use it have more than a pragmatic belief in its usefulness.[9] There is a wide range of technical systems in use, all based on the same basic proposition.

This proposition is that all fundamental factors are incorporated into the structure of prices, instantly discounted, and that prices obey patterns that

9 This intellectual foundation is stronger in the case of options, however, where what matters for prices is what people think matters for prices.

are wholly internal. Technical analysis, unlike fundamental analysis, does not rely on factors that are specific to one market or another; because prices are simply statistical variables, they follow patterns and display regularities that can be revealed by careful analysis. Some technical analysts describe their craft in more psychological terms, saying that market prices are the outcome of decisions by human traders, and that people tend to behave in similar ways in similar circumstances. The sum of a person's behaviour is the patterns and regularities in price.[10] There are many aspects to technical analysis, many of which can be combined into a trading system; that is, a set of rules that form a complete decision making set. These sets of rules are used by traders, and also are used by fund managers. There are very many extremely successful technically based funds; but they obviously do not reveal the exact nature of their trading rules.[11]

In the first place, there are a number of factors that can be considered to be guides to market psychology. Consider the volume and open interest statistics. These measure the volume of trading each day and the number of contracts at the end of each day that are still open. Open interest does not change when an existing holder of a long position sells his position to a new holder, but it does change when two new participants enter, one a long and one a short. If one takes the view that there is only a finite number of people (and a finite amount of money) interested in trading the markets, these statistics are revealing. For example, if prices and open interest rise together, the buying pressure is coming from new longs. In such a market, once volume begins to fall, it can be expected that the market has reached a temporary peak. Very high levels of open interest make a market vulnerable to reverse movements, since there are many people with open positions and these positions will have to be liquidated. Alternatively, if price and open interest fall, the selling pressure is coming from holders of long positions who are liquidating their positions. It does not come from new traders entering the market. This can be taken as an indication that there has been

10 The crux of the issue is whether prices are random variables or not. The 'random walk' view of prices (of commodities, or securities) has been hotly debated by economists for many years. The evidence is not compelling one way or another, although the latest research into the stock market does appear to be revealing evidence of 'mean reversion' in stock prices, which is not consistent with the random walk hypothesis. Part of the problem is the time scale over which prices are analyzed. Prices measured over a long period of time (for example annual prices measured over decades) may be random; hourly prices measured over a month may not.

11 Their success does not constitute evidence against the random walk hypothesis, since their trading rules may change and since their performance is not available over a long enough period of time.

no major change in market expectations; there are no new people wanting to enter the market, only people getting out of their positions.

It is important to note that each open position consists of one long and one short; it can never be the case that there are more longs than shorts. Only the direction of price change allows one to make deductions about who is driving the market. If prices fall and open interest rises, this is not because there are more shorts than longs; only that the selling pressure is coming from shorts, who are having to push prices lower in order to entice buyers into the market.

A further use of these figures is in conjunction with the Index of Bullish Market Opinion published by the weekly US magazine, Consensus. This index is the result of a survey of major brokerage house analysts and expresses prevailing market sentiment in the form of an index, bounded by zero and 100. High values are often called 'overbought' and low values 'oversold'; the idea being that, once the index reaches an extreme value, and everyone has the same opinion of the market, there can be no fresh trading activity to continue to move the market in that direction.

Once again, however, it is important to note that the underlying idea here is that there is a finite amount of money available to the market, and that price movements are like waves, with a constant ebb and flow of forces. This may well characterize day to day movements in ordinary market conditions, but clearly is not the case when market conditions change dramatically, as they do, for example, in drought conditions, when a lot of new money can be drawn into the market.[12]

A further refinement of these data comes with the data on the commitments of traders, provided for the US markets by the Commodity Futures Trading Commission. These reports monitor the positions of three groups of traders: hedgers, large speculators and non-reportable traders[13] usually taken to represent small speculators. This information is useful if one takes the view that large speculators and hedgers tend to be better informed than other traders. A major price change that has been associated with a large increase in hedging positions may well be the result of an increase in physical transactions. If prices have been going up, however, but large traders have been going short, the price rally is being driven by small speculators and therefore may not be well founded.

Another set of technical indicators that rely on the same basic approach are momentum indicators, such as the relative strength indicator, or RSI.

12 This is an illustration of a more general point; to the extent that technical analysis relies on the analysis of patterns, it will tend to get things wrong when a major change occurs in a market, unless, of course, the system changes and starts looking at the patterns revealed in unusual times.

13 These are the categories used by the CFTC, pursuant to its statutory obligations.

This indicator works very well in a market where there are regular cycles, with prices moving between peaks and troughs. It is calculated in the following way, usually with fourteen days of data, but any number of days can be used.

$$RSI = 100(RS/(1+RS))$$

RS is the weighted average of daily price increases in the past 14 days divided by the weighted average of daily price declines. The weights are calculated to give greater importance to recent days.

Other technical indicators are essentially ways of following trends and changes in trends. Identifying a trend can be as simple as looking at a chart of prices and relying on visual inspection. A more complex way is to calculate moving averages; these simply take out a lot of the 'noise' in daily price fluctuations. There is an old adage in the markets, 'the trend is your friend'; this expresses the view that a price trend should be followed, with a long or a short position, until the trend is exhausted. This poses the greatest problem for technical systems, how to tell when a trend has been broken. Since prices do move up and down even in a strongly trending market, how can one tell a normal daily fluctuation from a change in trend?

Moving averages can be used; the crossing of moving averages of different lengths (for example the nine and fifteen day moving averages) is often taken as an indication of such a change. Similarly, the momentum indicators can also be used. Chart analysis is perhaps the most commonly used method, however. Chart analysis is simply visual inspection of the patterns made by prices on a chart. The most common type of chart is a daily bar chart, on which each day's price movements are presented as a line connecting the day's high with the day's low. Sometimes a small tick to the left is used to indicate the day's opening price, and one to the right to indicate the closing price. With such a chart, it is obviously quite easy to see when prices are forming a trend. Changes in trend are often thought to be signalled by characteristic chart patterns. Perhaps the most famous is the 'head and shoulders' formation, in which prices rise to a peak, fall back, rise again above the first peak to form the 'head', fall back and then rise to the level of the first peak, to form the second 'shoulder'. At this point, with the market having fallen back from three rises, there is said to be strong evidence that the market has run out of steam and will fall back. Other patterns that are looked for are 'wedges', 'flags' and 'pennants', 'island tops' and 'island bottoms' and 'key reversals'. It often appears to the uninitiated (and the sceptical) that looking for patterns on a chart is not unlike looking at tea leaves to divine the future.

How do technical and fundamental analysis compare as useful trading tools? Fundamental analysis can often offer no help as to when to initiate a trade, and is not terribly useful when the key source of instability is on the supply side, since it is much easier to develop an econometric model that is sensitive to changes on the demand side than one that deals with supply shocks such as droughts. Technical analysis has the weakness that it can generate a lot of false trading signals, but its great advantage is that it can reveal a great deal about market psychology, and about what people think is important about price levels. Such factors cannot be ignored.

The regulation of futures trading

Like other financial market activities, futures trading is regulated by the authorities. In fact, the great bulk of regulation of trading is conducted by the exchanges themselves, since they determine the day-to-day 'rules of the game' and have established mechanisms for the settlement of disputes. There are very many disputes between traders that get resolved quickly by these procedures. Regulation in the broader sense of involvement by the public authorities is extensive, however.

In general, regulation is only economically justified when unregulated markets lead to socially undesirable outcomes. In financial markets, there are two kinds of market failure that justify public intervention. The first is asymmetric information. Trading companies and brokers know a lot more about the workings of futures markets than do members of the investing public, and the public has a right to be protected from unscrupulous people posing as investment advisors. It is often felt that this danger is greater in the futures markets because the possibility of leveraging investments, with the implied possibility of huge profits, can make people a little less cautious than they should be. This quality control function could, in principle, be left to the markets themselves, but is probably better entrusted to disinterested parties. It is needed because, without the confidence of the public, there would probably not be a volume of speculative interest in the markets large enough to allow them to perform their economic roles. To the extent that the economy as a whole has an interest in seeing that there are free and fair markets determining prices, regulation cannot be left to the markets themselves.

The second key problem is that of financial system collapse. Financial markets lie at the heart of the economy, and distress in the financial system can cause extremely serious problems; the example of the Great Depression shows this quite clearly.

The danger with public regulation of markets is that it can be excessive, stifling the innovation and entrepreneurship that a market system needs to flourish. Indeed, there have been repeated outright bans on futures trading at different times; futures trading in onions was banned in the US in 1958 and is still illegal; Japan prohibited all futures trading in 1868, and in Germany from 1896 to 1900 all futures trading was banned. But there is an equal danger with lax regulation; this provides an environment where fraud can flourish and the public loses confidence in market institutions.

The general trend in financial market regulation in the 1980s has been one of liberalization and harmonization. Developments in commodity futures markets have not been as dramatic as in markets for securities and for financial futures, but there certainly have been important changes. The approaches to regulation taken by the US and the UK are rather different, and provide a good illustration of the problems in this area.

In the US, futures market regulation is provided by the Commodity Futures Trading Commission (CFTC), which, in 1975, replaced the older Commodity Exchange Authority. This older body was under the authority of the Department of Agriculture, since futures trading used to be primarily in agricultural goods. The growth in financial futures trading made a move from the USDA sensible. The CFTC has two main purposes, and it has a wide range of legal powers to enforce its views. The first of these purposes is to ensure that futures trading meets its underlying purpose. Hence it has power to approve the operating rules of an exchange and to approve any new contract before it begins trading. It also monitors positions held by traders and can impose limits on these positions. The purpose of this is to prevent market manipulation.

Secondly, the CFTC regulates the dealings of the futures industry with the general public. Thus it imposes minimum standards of training of brokerage personnel, has capital adequacy standards for brokers and demands the segregation of clients' from firms' funds.

The CFTC is far too small to monitor all US exchanges all the time, but it does intervene in the markets frequently. Often its decisions are challenged in court by the exchanges themselves; it operates within a clear legal framework and people who think they have been unfairly treated by it can take it to court.

There has been a long running dispute between the CFTC and the Securities and Exchange Commission (SEC), the body responsible for the regulation of securities markets in the US. It has long been thought anomalous that trading in stocks should be regulated by one body whereas trading in stock index futures should be regulated by another. This sentiment was particularly marked after the October 1987 stock market crash, when there was debate over the role played by the futures market in the market decline. It seems likely that some redefinition of responsibilities between the two bodies will be inevitable, although the Chicago exchanges, whose lobbying power in Washington is formidable, have expressed a strong preference to remain under the authority of the CFTC, which they view as regulating with a lighter hand than the SEC.

In the UK, on the other hand, regulation was traditionally left to the exchanges themselves, with general supervision provided by the Bank of England. The sense that there was inadequate protection for investors led to the Gower Report on Investor Protection, whose principal recommendations were incorporated into the Financial Services Act of 1986. This set up the Securities and Investments Board (SIB) as the central regulatory authority for British financial markets. But the SIB's main role was to oversee the establishment of a network of self-regulatory organizations (SROs) which were to draw up rules governing the conduct of their members. In April 1988 it became illegal to carry out financial services without being a member of the relevant SRO. In the case of futures trading, the SRO when the law came into effect was the Association of Futures Brokers and Dealers (AFBD), although it subsequently merged with the Securities Association (which originally regulated trading in securities) to form the Securities and Futures Authority (SFA).

Since this regulatory system is new, it is still going through changes. In particular, the SIB is retreating from its earlier insistence on clear and unambiguous rules for every kind of transaction, on the grounds that this resulted in excessively detailed regulation, and developing instead a reliance on 'general principles' of dealing honestly with clients. With such regulatory changes, it is hard to reach conclusions about the UK system, but two important features of it stand out.

In the first place, there is no place in the UK framework for the general economic interest. Unlike the US system, it does not seek to advance the interest of the economy as a whole in having efficient financial markets. Cannot the markets on their own be expected to do this? Here the answer is no, for the following reason. The SROs contain in their rule books the now infamous 'fit and proper' clause, creating as a condition of membership of any SRO that a person be 'fit and proper' to carry out business. Nowhere are the determinants of fitness and propriety spelled out, with the result that this clause can be invoked to keep the industry in effect a gentlemen's club. Private cartels operated for the benefit of their members are not in the public interest, and existing participants in the financial services industry have every interest in erecting barriers to entry. Lack of competition from new entrants boosts their profit margins.

There is some evidence that this is how the UK regulatory regime is working. AFBD membership was denied in 1988 and 1989 to a number of futures brokers specializing in private client business; the 'fit and proper' clause was invoked. But as if to demonstrate that these decisions were not the actions of a private cartel, prosecutions were initiated against a number of people involved with these companies. The first prosecution to go to court involved a company known as DPR, three of whose directors were charged with a number of offences. The key allegation was of fraud against their clients. They were acquitted, however, after a case that the press estimated had cost over one million pounds.[14] Prosecutions against individuals from other firms were quietly dropped, but by then most of these firms had gone out of business, lacking the resources for a prolonged legal battle. The fact that the DPR case resulted in acquittal showed that there really was no justification for the AFBD's decision to exclude these firms from membership.

The regulatory regime in the UK, therefore, leaves a little to be desired, leaving the broader public interest to be defended only by the Bank of England and running the risk that market regulation becomes the preservation of a private cartel, restricting new entrants to the business from providing competition. Returns to companies operating in the financial markets should be determined by the markets, not by artificial barriers to entry.[15]

14 See Financial Times, *City traders acquitted*, July 13th 1990.

15 As this book went to press, questions of the adequacy of the Bank of England's regulatory oversight were being raised in the light of its decision to close the Bank of Credit and Commerce International in July 1991. Again, the key questions concerned the lack of an effective public interest dimension to regulation.

PART

IV

Looking ahead

CHAPTER

11

Market trends for the nineties

Looking ahead in markets is fraught with difficulty, and anyone who has ever spent time forecasting agricultural markets is probably more keenly aware of the difficulties than others. Nonetheless, there are a number of important issues that face grain markets, and one can at least delineate these issues and consider some likely outcomes. This falls short of formal forecasting of key variables, but it should throw some light on the years ahead.

Of course, there is always the unpredictable. In the late 1960s, few people thought the Soviet Union would emerge as a major grain importer, or that developing countries would become significant players in commercial grain markets. One should keep in mind the capacity of the world to generate surprises.

One prediction that can be made with a high degree of confidence is that grain prices will remain volatile. Cycles of boom and bust have been commonplace since the emergence of the modern grain economy, and there is no reason to believe that these cycles are a thing of the past. The boom of the 1920s was followed by the severe depression of the 1930s; high grain prices in the 1970s brought prosperity to many grain farmers, but the 1980s saw real prices hit new lows and a serious farm crisis, especially in North America.

The inherent variability in the weather is part of the explanation of price volatility, but there are other important factors. Oil prices affect grains because farmers use both energy and fertilizer derived from oil. Nearly 30% of the grain price rise of the 1970s was the result of higher oil prices. Agricultural policies imposed by major exporters and importers are also a major influence. To the extent that national policies seek to insulate every country's producers from the vicissitudes of the world market, the world market will tend to become more and more a residual market, with unstable and, eventually, meaningless prices. As seen in Chapter 3, the Uruguay Round of GATT talks sought to bring agricultural trade under the mantle of the GATT, a move that would in effect limit national autonomy in agricultural policy. In principle, this would result in an improved market, with a better allocation of resources in grain production. The possibility of trade liberalization is the first of the key issues for the nineties that shall be discussed.

Policy and trade liberalization

The fact that agricultural liberalization has appeared on the international agenda has released a flood of analytical work examining what would happen if liberalization were to occur.[1] In general, this analysis suggests that grain prices would be higher and that the EC would cease to be a major exporter under free trade. Consumers in developed countries would lose; producers in developing countries would gain. Producers in Canada and Australia would also be significant beneficiaries.

But this economic analysis takes the GATT talks rather too seriously, in that it attaches too high a probability to agricultural trade liberalization. The importance that the US placed on agricultural issues in the Uruguay Round reflected most importantly the sharp decline in its share of world grain markets in the 1980s, itself primarily the result of the growth of the EC's wheat surplus. The mounting budgetary costs of farm policies on both sides of the Atlantic have also had a salutary effect on thinking in both Washington and Brussels. While the US continued to insist on greater liberalization, and support for this position came from the Cairns Group (a group of 13 farm exporting nations), the commitment by the leaders of the seven major industrialized nations at the Houston Summit in 1990 to resolve the farm trade row failed to cower the farm lobby in the EC. This suggests that there

1 See in particular the works by Tyers and Anderson given in the bibliography, Goldin and Knudsen, (Ed), *Agricultural trade liberalization*, Devadross et al, *FAPRI trade model for wheat*, Liu and Roningen, *The world grains-oilseeds-livestock model*, Mitchell, *A world grains and soybeans model*, and Schiff, *An econometric analysis of the world wheat market*.

are two likely scenarios, both of which stop short of major liberalization. The first is that the US and the Cairns Group fail to achieve a satisfactory outcome and walk away from the talks. The growing attention being paid to the economic position of the Soviet Union and global environmental issues suggests that the political will to resolve farm trade disputes is lacking. On this scenario, grain markets would continue to see subsidy 'wars' between the EC and the US, at least until world market conditions become more favourable to exporters.

The second scenario is one in which a deal will eventually be cut between these two countries, a deal that meets the two imperatives of cutting the budgetary costs of farm policies and allowing the US to regain some market share. The internal (budgetary) pressure on the EC to make reforms is considerable, and the Commission has made a number of proposals for reform. These reforms do not promise significant liberalization of trade, but to the extent that production of grains is reduced (irrespective of the mechanisms used to accomplish this) the exportable surplus will be reduced and thus the conflict with the US lessened. This kind of deal is surely the most likely; the EC could claim it had retained the right to protect its farmers, and the US would be able to claim that the impact on the world market of the EC's policies had been significantly reduced.

Whatever the outcome of the trade talks, agricultural policy will remain extremely important for grain markets. Outside a few free market think tanks dotted around the world, there is little interest in complete liberalization of agriculture. One can hope for a steady move towards policies that distort resource allocation as little as possible, but the workings of agricultural policy will undoubtedly remain a significant influence on grain production, consumption, marketing and prices.

Agricultural policy in the EC is also likely to emerge as an important issue in the transformation of Eastern Europe. Several of the formerly socialist countries can be expected to become significant agricultural exporters; indeed, Hungary already is one. At present, the EC's restrictions on imports of agricultural goods are depriving these countries of valuable opportunities to exercise their comparative advantage; and the EC's aggressive export subsidies are also limiting the incentives to the region's farmers to expand their production. In this area, as in many others, the EC's preference is for aid channelled through governmental or official agencies (such as the newly established European Bank for Reconstruction and Development) rather than for open markets and the benefits that trade brings.[2]

2 Meanwhile, the World Bank has estimated that industrial countries' trade barriers against imports from developing countries cost developing countries as much as they receive in aid from the rich countries.

The Soviet Union and China

There is no clearer illustration of the impact of the policy environment on agriculture generally and grain in particular than the Soviet Union and China. These two countries have had a pronounced impact on world grain markets over the past 20 years. A good part of the variability in grain trade and grain prices can be explained by their importing behaviour. They will also be important for the 1990s.

The Soviet Union

In the case of the Soviet Union, the key question concerns the possible realization of its agricultural potential. Despite the environmental damage wrought on vast areas of prime agricultural land by inappropriate applications of pesticides and herbicides and by a lack of soil conservation, the USSR boasts some of the best land in the world. What is more, its agricultural failings have been at least as large in the organization of the marketing chain as in production, suggesting the scope for improvement is even greater. Can this potential be realized?

The ideological barriers to improved production and marketing have now largely disappeared. These barriers were, historically, of great importance; the massive investments in state and collective farms, based on the idea that only social ownership of land and other assets could allow economies of scale to be captured, ran counter to the emphasis on local decision making and individual responsibility that lie at the heart of successful agricultural production systems. Pricing policies that were little short of bizarre discouraged the timely co-ordination and efficient use of inputs as diverse as pesticides and spares for machinery, and led, in the case of grain, to poor feed conversion rates. The effective abandonment of the ideological commitment to socialist agriculture allows one to envisage a future in which Soviet farming's productivity will increase, since it could be organized on the basis of smaller, more flexible, locally-managed units responding to market prices.

Unfortunately for the Soviet people, this prospect is not likely to be realized in the 1990s. There are two main reasons for this. In the first place, although the commitment to a centrally planned economy has been abandoned, at time of writing nothing has been put in its place. This policy vacuum has allowed some entrepreneurs to flourish, in agriculture as in other areas, but it does not represent the kind of environment in which investment for a longer term return is likely to take place. For every entrepreneur taking advantage of the situation there is a party bureaucrat trying to hold back change. A stronger domestic consensus on what kind of agricultural system is wanted will be required before a response can be expected.

Secondly, the current asset configuration is so distorted that it will take a long time to correct it. Soviet farm labour tends to be highly specialized, when Western farms typically employ labour with general skills. Collectivization took place so long ago that there is, to all intents and purposes, no living memory and experience of independently managed farms. Similarly, there is too much heavy machinery on Soviet farms, designed to exploit economies of scale that simply do not exist (and certainly do not exist on the smaller farms that are the norm in private agriculture).

This is not to say that there cannot be a sudden improvement in the Soviet agricultural position; it seems clear that changes in the marketing chain could be introduced fairly quickly and that they would have a rapid pay off. But the emergence of an efficient and highly productive farm sector in the Soviet Union will require years of investment in human capital and better institutions, in the context of sensible economic policies. This task has only just begun.

It is not necessarily an implication of the above that the USSR will continue to be a large importer of grain. As economic reforms are introduced, grain imports are likely to be constrained by the Soviets' limited ability to finance these imports. Declining oil production (and weak oil prices, despite the temporary boost caused by the Iraqi invasion of Kuwait and the subsequent conflict), mounting foreign indebtedness and growing concerns about political stability were already affecting the country's creditworthiness in early 1991. The lower consumer incomes that are inevitable during the reform process will also dampen demand for meat (and hence for feedgrains). It may also be the case that disputes between the component republics will limit the free flow of grain from the country's ports to its agricultural hinterland. For all these reasons, the outlook to the mid-1990s at least is for levels of imports that are quite modest by the standards of the early 1980s.

China

China presents a completely different set of problems. It is quite widely touted as an example of successful agricultural reform. In 1978, a series of reforms were initiated, marking the beginning of a period of radical agricultural reform. These reforms led to a sharp increase in the country's grain production.[3] Despite these successes, and the potential for further increases in production, and despite the government's stated policy of grain

3 In one important way, Chinese agriculture differs from that in the Soviet Union; collectivization was much later, and the peasants retained direct experience of managing their plots. Hence they were much better placed to take advantage of a more liberal policy framework.

self-sufficiency, it is widely expected that Chinese grain imports will grow significantly in the 1990s. There will continue to be year-to-year fluctuations, but there are a number of reasons for expecting import growth.

In the first place, China's financial position is not a serious constraint on its ability to finance whatever grain imports it needs. Although it faces a number of economic difficulties, they do not compare to those of the Soviet Union, nor does the country's political stability appear to be in doubt. Its balance of payments position and its creditworthiness will allow it to buy grain.

Secondly, the country's internal transportation system is such that coastal urban areas can be more cheaply served by imported grain. As these cities continue to grow (in both population and income terms), their imports will grow.

Thirdly, continued population growth, economic growth and urbanization are likely to lead to increases in demand beyond the capacity of domestic production to meet. Demand for feedgrains is particularly important in this context, since consumer demand for meat will grow and leave the Chinese with a growing deficit in feedgrains. Certainly, the investments (in plant breeding, in land reclamation, in irrigation, in fertilizer production, in transportation infrastructure) needed to increase production by enough to supply the likely domestic demand would have a large opportunity cost in terms of foregone industrial investments, and the Chinese may well decide that a greater reliance on imports is a better choice.

The role of developing countries

Another key issue for the 1990s is the role of the developing countries. We have seen how important they have become as importers of both wheat and coarse grains. There is no reason to expect that this importance will diminish: indeed, it is likely to grow. One of the more remarkable, but little remarked, changes in the world economy in the 1980s has been the switch away from interventionism towards more liberal economic policies throughout the developing world. The obvious success of the dynamic East Asian economies, the financial difficulties experienced by overburdened governments during the debt crisis and the manifest failure of the East European model of development have all had a profound influence on policy makers in developing countries. These changes in the general economic climate have two main implications for the grain market. In the first place, agricultural systems in many developing countries are being liberalized, creating the prospect of increased production and better marketing. The abolition of state-controlled marketing monopolies is also removing the grain marketing system from under the direct control of the state. This should make it easier for private companies to finance grain imports if they need to.

The second implication is through the effect on grain demand of the better economic performance that a better macroeconomic policy framework should promote. Developing countries are the countries with the highest population growth rates; if this population growth is combined with even moderately good economic performance, demand for grains can only grow. It has been seen earlier how rapid the growth in grain demand has been in rapidly industrializing countries; from the example of Britain's growth in the nineteenth century, to Japan's in the 1950s and 1960s, and, most recently, the examples of South Korea, Taiwan, Hong Kong and Singapore. No-one expects the example of the Asian dragons to be widely replicated, but in so far as developing countries grow, their demand for grain will also grow. The fruits of better macroeconomic policies take years to ripen, but there is already a second generation of Asian countries beginning to enjoy the kind of rapid growth rates that are a mark of success; Thailand, Malaysia and Indonesia are the most important. Thailand is a major food exporter, but grain consumption in all three is rising. The Pacific Rim will grow in importance to the grain economy over the 1990s.

This growth in Pacific Rim countries is a strong argument for the development of a futures trading facility somewhere in the region. The basis risks faced by Asian importers using the Chicago markets are considerable, and an exchange in the region would greatly facilitate the trade. There are a number of exchanges in the region; in Hong Kong, in Singapore, in Kuala Lumpur and, of course, in Japan, Australia and New Zealand. Most of these exchanges have experience with the trading of agricultural contracts, and it surely cannot be long before one of them begins to trade imported grains.

Implications for production, consumption and trade

What do these trends imply for production, consumption and trade over the 1990s? Obviously, the further to the future one looks, the greater the uncertainty, and no forecast can foresee the kind of dramatic developments, such as droughts or major policy changes, that have a major effect on the grain market. In the absence of any significant shock, the market is likely to have the following features.

EC production of wheat is likely to stabilize or only increase modestly. Although yields are likely to go up, planted areas are likely to fall slightly as policy changes are introduced to curb over production. In the other major exporters, wheat production is likely to increase; this increase could be marked in the second half of the decade in the USA, since in 1995 about 45 million acres of land currently enrolled in the Conservation Reserve Program will be available for cultivation. Despite the increase in production in exporters, trade is not likely to grow by much in the early part of the decade; indeed, the difficulties facing the Soviet Union could result in further contractions in imports. This suggests that world wheat prices are likely to remain low, with continued strong competition among exporters. Nonetheless, a deal is likely between the EC and the US under which the US will cease to lose market share in world wheat trade. This is most likely to happen if the EC further constrains its domestic market in order to impose greater use of wheat as an animal feed.

With coarse grains, the situation looks a little different. Although production is likely to continue to rise, increases in demand, particularly in East Asia, are likely to be strong enough to ensure growth in world trade and somewhat firmer prices. This could well encourage greater use of wheat as a feed in the period up to 1995.

As seen earlier, developing countries are likely to grow in importance to the grain market. This does have important implications for trade patterns, since developing countries tend to buy grain in smaller and more variable amounts. They also are more likely to experience credit difficulties. This is likely to increase the dominance of the large trading companies over the global grain trade, since their flexibility, size and information networks put them in a good position to deal with such a pattern of trade.

As one looks to the longer term, however, with growing demands for grain in developing countries, one is driven to consider the Malthusian constraint. Can the world keep on producing all the grain it needs?

A world food crisis ahead?

It was Thomas Malthus who first popularized the fear that population growth would exceed the capacity of land to feed people, leading to 'natural' checks on population, such as diseases, mass starvation or wars as nations competed for good land. His Essay on the Principle of Population was first published in 1798 but was so popular that Malthus published six editions, the last in 1826. The argument changed in a number of important respects over the course of the revisions, but the key claim can be seen in the first edition:

> I say that the power of population is indefinitely greater than the power of the earth to produce subsistence for man. Population, when unchecked, increases in a geometrical ratio. Subsistence only increases in an arithmetical

> ratio. A slight acquaintance with numbers will show the immensity of the first power in comparison with the second.

The argument, therefore, is that the rate of growth of population is greater than the rate of growth of food output. The popularity of Malthus' essay, and the notoriety it gained him, tell us something about the market for prognostications of gloom. Not surprisingly, similar claims can still be found in the literature: the World Watch Institute report, State of the World 1990, contains the following claims.

> The world's farmers are finding it more difficult to keep up with growth in population. (p4) . . . The world enters the nineties not only with a low level of grain in reserve, but with little confidence that the 'carryover' stocks can be rebuilt quickly. Sketching out the consequences of a poor harvest while stocks are this low sounds like the outline of a science fiction catastrophe novel. If before stocks are rebuilt the United States experiences a drought-reduced harvest similar to that of 1988, which dropped grain production below domestic consumption, grain exports will slow to a trickle . . . By early fall, the nearly 100 countries that import grain from the US would be competing for meager exportable supplies from Argentina, Australia and France. Fierce competition could double or triple grain prices, driving them far above any level previously experienced. (p11–12)

How seriously should such arguments be taken? In the first place, there is an obvious misperception that needs to be corrected. Anyone with even a casual familiarity with grain prices would not make the claim that a tripling in grain prices would send them above any level previously experienced. Refer back to Chapter 7, and particularly Fig. 7.1 where wheat and maize prices for the past century are presented. It would clearly take more than a tripling of grain prices to push prices above those within living memory. This is important, because prices are a measure of relative scarcity. The fact that real grain prices have been moving down for so long and reached record lows in the 1980s tells us that the supply of grain has been consistently growing more rapidly than effective demand.

The error in Malthus' original proposition was to believe that the coefficients governing the expansion of population and agricultural production were fixed, which they clearly are not. It is not surprising that he believed as he did, however, (people well into this century believed it also) that wheat yields were constant and that planted area was the only significant determinant of production. Moreover, there is t least some reason to believe that the rate of technical progress is itself endogenous, determined at least in part by the resources devoted to it (and thus influenced by prices). Another important factor that allowed Britain to escape the Malthusian constraint in the nineteenth century was trade: by specializing and engaging in trade, Britain was able to raise the number of people it could support on its small land area.

It should be borne in mind, however, that global figures tells very little about distribution. In Africa, the Malthusian theory is a lot closer to reality than it is in Europe or North America; even at the historically low levels of grain prices in the 1980s, grain was too expensive for many Africans. Low incomes have combined with political instability, poor policies and bad weather created severe famines on several occasions on the continent. In this sense, there is a food crisis with us now. But this is, above all, a political problem, and a problem of poverty. It is not a failure of the grain market.[4]

But the question remains; can world food output continue to grow at a faster rate than world population? The new concern here is really environmental degradation; the fear that global warming, soil erosion, falling soil fertility, lack of prospects for extending irrigated area and the adverse effects on plant growth of atmospheric pollutants will combine to defeat the best efforts of farmers to produce more food. What are the relevant facts?

In the first place, it should be noted that whatever difficulties the world may face over the longer term, there is no serious cause for concern for the next decade or so. Over the period 1970 to 1988, world wheat production grew at an average annual rate of about 2.8%, and most people expect it to grow by 2 to 2.5% over the period to 2000. With coarse grains, the figures are 1.8% and 2%. In the period 1970–88, production growth was slowest in the USSR and East Europe; even a modest improvement in the performance of these countries would improve the world outlook considerably. What is more, there is considerable excess capacity in grain markets at present; if there were not, the US and the EC would not be in such serious dispute in the GATT and their farmers would not need massive subventions from the public purse.

4 Amartya Sen, the Harvard economist who has made a detailed study of famines, points out that there has never been a famine in a country with a free press. See his comments at the 1991 World Bank Conference, listed under Sen in the bibliography (the remarks cited here can be found on page 424). In other words, politics determines whether a famine would be so costly to a government that it would take steps to prevent its occurrence. African political systems have frequently not had to face significant costs from allowing their people to starve. Anyway, the world produces more than enough food to feed Africa; that is not the point.

Over the longer term, is there cause for concern? World average grain yields per hectare rose by 26% in the 1960s, by 21% in the 1970s and by 20% in the 1980s. Although these are large figures, the rate of growth is dropping and they give rise to concern that a yield plateau may be approaching. The technological improvements of the 1960s (notably the 'Green Revolution') have by now been fully absorbed by the system, the argument goes, leaving little scope for further improvements. Meanwhile, ecological deterioration (which is extremely serious in some countries) threatens even the existing stock of land.[5]

It is, of course, true that, for any given technology, there is an implied yield plateau. The point about technology changes, however, is that they change the yield plateau: new technology makes possible what old technology did not permit. And it is inherent in new technology that one cannot foresee it; today's grain yields would have been inconceivable fifty years ago. In this case, the example of rice is perhaps most interesting, since some of these trends are clearer in the rice market. Moreover, the geographical concentration of rice production and its role in the diets of poor people make it an interesting case.

A major research effort by the International Rice Research Institute (IRRI) led to the creation of high yielding rice varieties as part of the Green Revolution.[6] These plants have now been widely adopted, but since adoption rates are so high, the growth rate of rice yields will inevitably fall. Indeed, there is some evidence that rice yields are reaching a plateau in Asia, whereas the plateau for average world wheat and coarse grains, given existing best practice, is still some way off. In Japan, for example, yields have hardly changed since 1970. Whether this matters depends on one's view of future technological change. A prominent rice breeder at IRRI, quoted in the World Bank's 1991 World Development Report, believes that 'existing techniques could be used to increase rice production by 25 to 30% over the next decade' and that research now in progress will lead to emergence of further improved

5 Global warming and its impact on agriculture have also been the subject of much discussion, particularly in the US. Very little is known about this process and even less about the impact on agriculture, and it would be wise to reserve judgement until more is known. On present knowledge, however, it does seem clear that there will be both winners and losers from the process; a northern shift in the world's grain belts would be bad news for the US (where the environmental lobby is loudest and expresses the greatest concern) but it is hard to see that global grain production would suffer; Canada, China and the USSR would all gain. A lot more is needed to be known about what global warming actually implies before a reasonable debate can be held on these subjects.

6 IRRI is part of a network of internationally funded agricultural research institutes, covering major crops and geographical areas.

varieties of rice with yields of 13–15 tonnes per hectare, compared to maximum yields with current varieties of 8–9 tonnes.[7]

More generally, there is the promise of biotechnology. The most intensive research efforts so far in this field have been in livestock husbandry, not crop production, but since livestock are such important consumers of grain, there are obvious implications for the grain market.

Fundamentally, there is no proof that technological progress will continue indefinitely to allow humanity to economize on land; it is a question of how one views history and whether one believes the current situation is qualitatively different from all history. In the past, the world's agriculturalists have been astonishingly inventive, innovative and dynamic in rising to challenges. There is little reason to believe this will change.

7 See the *World Development Report 1991*; particularly Box 4.1 in Chapter 4. Chapter 4 of the report contains a discussion of agricultural technology and presents an optimistic view of technological possibilities.

Appendix: the world rice market

The main body of this book concentrated on wheat and the major coarse grains. The exclusion of rice was justified because of the pronounced differences between these grains, on the one hand, and rice on the other. Rice is, however, an extremely important grain, albeit one whose production and trade patterns are unusual. Its importance can be very simply stated: it is the staple food of nearly half of the world's population. At the same time, its distinctiveness can be simply stated: Asia accounts for about 90% of the world's rice production and consumption. This appendix provides a brief overview of the rice market, to complement the analysis of wheat and coarse grains in the main body of the text.

Production

Rice was first cultivated in China around 2,800 BC and spread from there to India. From Asia it has spread to all regions of the world. It grows well in the temperate climates of Japan and Korea, even though it is often thought of as a tropical crop. It is grown on every continent, even though Asian production dwarfs that elsewhere. There are two principal types of rice grown.

Softer, rounder, short-grain rice is the preferred type in China, Japan and Korea; elsewhere, long-grain rice tends to be preferred.

Rice also differs from other grains in its requirements for processing before consumption. Once rice is harvested, it is said to be in the rough state. It then undergoes a process known as milling. Milled rice is the grain from which the husks and bran have been extracted, and at this stage it is ready for consumption. Although some rice, like wheat, is ground into flour for further processing, the quantities involved are small. The milling process does remove a large amount of weight: husks account for between 20 and 25% of the weight of rough rice, and the bran for a further 5 to 8%. Hence production, when expressed on a milled basis, is lower than paddy production by as much as one third.

World rice production has been growing steadily over the past 30 years; the annual average growth rate over the period 1961–1990 was 3%. This is in line with the production growth rates achieved by wheat and coarse grains. Production in 1990 was 508 million tonnes (rough basis), equivalent to 344 million tonnes on a milled basis. Table A.1 shows the breakdown of this production by the major producing countries. It can be readily seen that China is by far the world's largest producer. China and India together account for more than half of world production.

The dominance of Asia producers points to a significant feature of rice production. After all, Asia is the most densely populated continent, with little land available for agricultural expansion. The production increase that has been seen over the past 30 years has been primarily the result of improvements in yields. In the mid-1960s, rice was harvested on about 125 million hectares of land. The harvested area had risen to 143 million hectares by 1975, but has grown very little since then. In 1990, harvest area was 147 million hectares. Conversely, yields have risen steadily, from around two tons per hectare (rough basis) in the early 1960s to 3.5 tons per hectare in the most recent past.

Table A.1 World rice production (million metric tons, rough basis)

	1984	**1985**	**1986**	**1987**	**1988**	**1989**	**1990**
China	168.9	178.3	168.5	171.1	173.9	169.1	180.1
India	90.2	87.5	96.2	90.0	85.3	105.7	111.1
Indonesia	35.3	38.1	39.0	38.4	41.5	42.3	44.7
Thailand	19.5	19.9	19.7	18.0	18.0	21.3	20.2
Bangladesh	21.8	21.9	22.6	23.2	23.1	23.3	26.8
World total	453.8	468.4	470.9	465.8	463.5	488.8	508.1

This yield improvement is primarily the result of the Green Revolution, and the improved, high-yielding varieties (HYVs) of rice that it made available. It has been convincingly demonstrated that these HYVs produce higher yields when they are adequately provided with water and fertilizer. Absent these key inputs, they are less resilient than unimproved rice varieties. The increase in rice production, therefore, has been linked to the increase in irrigated area; that is, the kind of conditions under which HYVs can deliver their promise. Variations in yield from one country to another are largely explained by variations in the proportion of the rice crop that is grown under controlled water conditions. In some countries, for example, China and South Korea, over 90% of the rice land is irrigated. In the US, the whole of the rice crop is irrigated.

Consumption

Asians dominate rice consumption. Annual per capita rice consumption in Asia is approximately 100 kilograms, compared to under four kilograms in Western Europe and North America. Virtually all of this is consumed as direct human food. It was George Bernard Shaw who remarked that most people live in Asia; one can add to this and say that most poor people live in Asia. Rice is extremely important in the diets of the Asian poor. Demand for rice has been closely correlated with the growth in population in Asia; but there is also some evidence that rising incomes have tended to reduce demand for rice. Just as people in the West tend to eat less bread (and more meat, fruits and vegetables) as they get richer, so people in Asia tend to eat less rice and to consume more bread, meat, fruits and vegetables. In Japan, for example, per capita rice consumption peaked at 140 kilograms per year in 1920, and has been declining ever since; to 125 kilograms in the early 1960s and to 85 kilograms by the late 1980s. Similarly, other rapidly growing Asian countries, such as Malaysia, Singapore, Taiwan and Thailand have seen their per capita consumption levels fall quite consistently since the early 1960s. This is not a wholly consistent trend, since per capita consumption has gone up in other countries, notably China, Indonesia and the Philippines; but these countries are considerably poorer. It seems likely that, when people are very poor, an income increase leads to higher levels of rice consumption, but, after they have reached a certain level, further income increases cause them to switch out of rice and towards more 'Western' foods. Income elasticities are around 0.1 for Indonesia, China and the Philippines, but they are negative for most other Asian countries; around −0.02 for Bangladesh but around −0.6 for Malaysia and Singapore.[1]

1 Elasticities are also declining over time. See Shoichi Ito et al: 'Rice in Asia: Is it becoming an inferior good?', *American Journal of Agricultural Economics*, Vol. 71, No. 1, February 1989, pp. 32–42.

Table A.2 presents summary data on rice consumption (on a milled basis; this explains why world consumption is so much lower than the world production, on a rough basis, given in Table A.1). Again, China dominates the picture, accounting for one third of world consumption and, China and India, together account for more than half of the world figure.

Table A.2 World rice consumption (million metric tons, milled basis)

	1984	1985	1986	1987	1988	1989	1990
China	117.1	123.9	117.2	119.5	123.3	121.6	123.1
India	58.2	56.7	62.4	61.3	59.3	65.7	71.6
Indonesia	25.3	25.2	26.2	26.6	27.2	28.2	28.2
World total	308.7	313.8	316.4	320.6	320.0	328.6	337.5

Another striking feature of the data is the volatility of consumption in India and China. Although world consumption has been on a reasonably stable path, consumption in these two major countries has fluctuated quite widely from one year to the next. In 1984, Chinese consumption was 117 million tonnes. It rose to 124 million in 1985, only to fall back to 117 in 1986.

The importance of rice to the diets of the poor (and, of course, as a source of income for farmers) has led Asian governments to take a very active role in their countries' rice markets. Government intervention takes many forms, and ranges from price controls to restrictions on international trade and includes government control of marketing.

Exports and Imports

One aspect of this has been the extensive implementation of policies of self-sufficiency. The commitment to self-sufficiency is not confined to the governments of poor countries: the consistent refusal of Japan to lift its import restrictions on rice has been a major irritant in US/Japanese relations. Japan's various justifications for the continued ban on imports have ranged from the mystical (such as the claim that rice occupies a special place in Japanese culture) to the bizarre (such as the claim that Japanese stomachs are different from those elsewhere) but the policy has not been one that any Japanese government has appeared likely to change. The generous supports to rice farming, coupled with the declining per capita consumption noted above, have resulted in the emergence of an export surplus of rice. In poorer countries, self-sufficiency policies have not yet reached this level of idiocy, but they have been very widely adopted. A consequence of this is that international trade is very limited in extent. In contrast to wheat and coarse grains, only about 5% of the world's rice crop enters international trade. Table A.3 presents data on recent imports of rice.

Table A.3 World rice imports (thousand metric tons, milled basis)

	1984	1985	1986	1987	1988	1989	1990
EC	1,246	1,259	1,326	1,090	1,210	1,263	1,204
Iran	730	600	450	850	400	1,000	850
Saudi Arabia	530	500	500	500	431	525	525
Malaysia	437	480	325	375	350	360	360
USSR	150	150	200	200	498	600	400
World	12,558	11,475	12,739	11,955	11,930	15,101	12,044

It is very interesting that none of the main consuming nations is a significant importer and that the world's largest importer is the European Community. Rice, of course, is not a staple in Europe. Iran has recently emerged as a large importer, and Saudi Arabia has been a large and consistent importer for many years. But of the major consuming countries in South and East Asia, none is an important importer. It can also be deduced from the table that there are very few markets of any size. A very large number of countries import rice, but on a very small scale. Data on world exports, presented in Table A.4, also show a number of surprises.

Table A.4 World rice exports (thousand metric tons, milled basis)

	1984	1985	1986	1987	1988	1989	1990
Thailand	4,528	3,993	4,338	3,700	4,791	6,037	3,927
US	2,129	1,906	2,401	2,400	2,247	2,973	2,424
Pakistan	1,050	962	1,146	1,300	950	779	904
China	1,168	1,010	950	900	698	320	300
EC	763	885	1,136	1,045	920	963	969
Vietnam	150	50	50	50	97	1,400	1,500
World	12,558	11,475	12,739	11,955	11,930	15,101	12,044

Thailand is the world's most important exporter, accounting for about one third of world shipments. Interestingly, the second most important exporter is the US, hardly one of the world's most important rice producing and consuming nations. These two countries have consistently accounted for more than half of world exports. Another interesting feature of the table is the growth of Vietnam as a rice exporter. Less than five years ago, its exports were insignificant, yet it now has a substantial export surplus. Not surprisingly, this development reflects a change in domestic economic policies and, in particular, the abandonment of some of the key features of socialist agriculture. Families can now take out long term leases on land; private ownership of animals and equipment is permitted; and restrictions have been lifted on the private marketing of both inputs and grain. Vietnamese farmers have responded to the opportunities opened up by this liberalization and have started to produce more rice than the country can consume. China has also been a large exporter in the past, but the swings in export levels reflect changes in the central government's agricultural policies. In the past, rice was exported primarily as a way of earning foreign exchange; there have been times when the Chinese exported rice and imported wheat, taking advantage of the rice:wheat price ratio to lower the cost at which food was delivered to the population. More recently, greater provincial authority over grain trade has allowed some rice-deficit provinces to import directly rather than rely on other provinces. This has had the effect of reducing China's net exports quite considerably.

Rice marketing and prices

Not surprisingly, the marketing channels for rice differ from those for wheat and coarse grains. Again, this reflects the higher degree of government

Table A.5 Milled rice prices: 5% brokens, FOB Bangkok (US dollars per metric ton)

Year	Price
1970	144
1971	129
1972	147
1973	350
1974	542
1975	363
1976	255
1977	272
1978	368
1979	334
1980	434
1981	483
1982	293
1983	277
1984	252
1985	216
1986	210
1987	230
1988	301
1989	320
1990	287

Source: Economic Research Service, USDA.

involvement in the market. The control of trade channels by governments means that a very large proportion of international trade in rice is conducted on a government-to-government basis. Industrial country exporters ship a large part of their rice exports under various concessional programmes. A consequence of this is that the genuinely private trade in rice is very limited in extent.

Moreover, the 'world market', that is the freely traded part of the market, is very much a residual market, in that it is small in extent and it can easily be swamped by very small changes in one of the major producers. For this reason, world market prices are very unstable. The price that is usually taken to be the reference price for world trade is the price for milled Thai rice, since Thailand is the major exporter. But it is not at all clear that this price represents any transactions of real economic significance. Table A.5 above shows annual rice prices since 1970. In broad terms, prices have followed the same general trends as other grains: one can clearly see the rise in the early 1970s, and another rise in the late 1980s. It is also worth noting that rice is, in absolute terms, much more expensive than wheat, although its premium is eroding.

Key Issues for the 1990s

The foregoing brief overview of the rice market illustrated the many ways in which it differs markedly from wheat and coarse grains. For the future, however, many of the key issues faced in the rice market are similar to those faced in the markets for other grains. One key uncertainty surrounds China. Chinese production is so large in relation to world production, that any significant change in Chinese rice policies would have a major impact. A decision to export more would, in all likelihood, depress world market prices; conversely, the growth of import dependence would challenge the capacity of existing exporters. Incomes in China appear to be at the level where an increase would stimulate demand for rice; yet the country has limited opportunities for further expanding the area on which rice is grown.

Similar issues arise in other developing Asian economies. The extent to which consumption will grow will vary from one country to another, but demand is likely to rise, not least because population growth will, for Asia as a whole, counteract the impact of a negative income elasticity. It is possible that these growing demands will pose a threat to established policies of self-sufficiency and cause the emergence of a large import requirement. This is all the more pressing, since the basis of many self-sufficiency policies has been the kind of government subsidies (for fertilizer, for example) that are now being phased out around the world. This focuses attention on what is perhaps the most commonly discussed issue among analysts of the rice market: what is the outlook for continuing increases in rice yields?

This issue has risen to prominence because of the appearance of a 'yield plateau' in Asia, as the new technology introduced in the 1960s has been fully adopted by the system. Yet it is not clear that pessimism is warranted. In the first place, it may not be the case that gains from existing technology have been exhausted. Although the impetus to world yields given by the Green Revolution appears to have passed, with HYVs widely adopted, one should not forget that farmers operate under economic as well as technological constraints. The example of Vietnam in recent years shows what gains can be made, with existing technology, once production is organized in a sensible way. Few countries have as much room for improvement as Vietnam had, but improvements in marketing systems could certainly increase production in a large number of countries. It should also be borne in mind that farmers in many developing countries have received only a rudimentary education; improved education levels would make it easier to ensure the adoption of yield-enhancing management and agronomic practices. These gains in yields can be realized without new rice varieties.

Over the longer term, however, the ability of rice production to continue to grow must depend on further technological progress. The International Rice Research Institute is continuing to work on this issue, and its scientists are optimistic about the possibility of further advances. Biotechnology holds obvious promise. Many people do feel, however, that any significant technological breakthrough is at least a decade away. This suggests that, at least over the medium term, increases in demand in major markets will have to be met by imports rather than domestic production. There seems little doubt that exporters could expand production (if it were profitable to do so); partly because they can shift land into rice from other crops more easily than other producers, and partly because there are known technologies (for example hybrid seed, that produces a higher yield yet requires good conditions, a functioning market and distribution system for seed and a large labour force) that some exporters could adopt to increase production.

The existence of medium term constraints on the ability of key consumers to increase production suggests that one of two things might occur. The first is a set of deliberate policies to encourage the shift in consumption away from rice and towards grains that will be abundantly available on the world market. The second is that governments of consuming countries might begin to rely more heavily on imports as a way of meeting domestic demand. If that occurs, then the rice market will begin to look a little less unusual and a little more like the markets for wheat and coarse grains.

Bibliography

Alexandratos N (Ed): 'World agriculture toward 2000; an FAO study'. New York, New York University Press, 1988.

Anderson K and Tyers R: 'European Community grain and meat policies: effects on international prices, trade and welfare', *European Review of Agricultural Economics*, Vol 11, No 4, 1984, pp 367–394.

Anderson K and Tyers R: 'Global effects of liberalising trade in agriculture'. Aldershot, Gower Publishing for the Trade Policy Research Centre, 1988.

Andrae G and Beckman B: 'The wheat trap'. London, Zed Books, 1986.

Atkin M: 'Agricultural commodity markets: a guide to futures trading'. London, Routledge, 1989.

Benedict M R: 'Farm policies of the United States, 1790–1950', New York, The Twentieth Century Fund, 1953.

Blandford D: 'Instability in world grain markets'. *Journal of Agricultural Economics*, Vol 34, No. 3, September 1988, pp 379–395.

Boatfield G: 'Farm crops'. Ipswich, Farming Press, 1979.

Bond G and Thompson S R: 'Basis and exchange rate risk in offshore futures trading', *American Journal of Agricultural Economics*, Vol 67, No 5, December 1985, pp 980–985.

Boussard J M: 'A French perspective on supply control and management', *Journal of Agricultural Economics*, Vol 39, No 3, September 1988, pp 326–340.

Braudel F: 'Civilization and capitalism 15th–18th centuries: volume 2. The wheels of commerce'. New York, Harper & Row, 1982.

Butler N: 'The international grain trade: problems and prospects'. London, Croom Helm, 1986.

Byerlee D and Sain G: 'Food pricing policy in developing countries: bias against agriculture or for urban consumers?' *American Journal of Agricultural Economics*, Vol 68, No 4, November 1986, pp 961-969.

Carter C and Schmitz A: 'Import tariffs and price formation in the international wheat market', *American Journal of Agricultural Economics*, Vol 61, No 3, August 1979, pp 517-522.

Carter C A and Zhong Fu-Ning: 'China's grain production and trade: an economic analysis'. Boulder, Westview Press, 1988.

Commonwealth Secretariat: 'Variable exchange rates and trading on commodity markets'. Commonwealth Economic Papers Number 20, London, January 1986.

Cooke C and Sundquist W B, 'Cost efficiency in US corn production', *American Journal of Agricultural Economics*, Vol 71, No 4, November 1989, pp 1003-1010.

Cramer G L and Heid W G Jr: 'Grain marketing economics'. New York, John Wiley & Sons, 1983.

Davies J K: 'Democracy and classical Greece'. London, Fontana, 1978.

Devadross S, Helmar M and Meyers W: 'FAPRI trade model for wheat: specification, estimation and validation'. Center for Agricultural and Rural Development (CARD) Staff report 86-SR2, Iowa State Univerity, Ames, Iowa, 1986.

Fornari H: 'Bread upon the waters'. Nashville, Aurora Publishers, 1973.

Freivalds J: 'Grain trade'. New York, Stein & Day, 1976.

Furtan W H *et al:* 'Grain market outlook, Ottawa' Economic Council of Canada, 1989.

Gallagher P: 'The grain sector of the European Community: policy formation, price determination and implications for trade', *American Journal of Agricultural Economics*, Vol 70, No 4, November 1988, pp 767-778.

Gardner B L: 'Rollover hedging and missing long term futures markets', *American Journal of Agricultural Economics*, Vol 71, No 2, May 1989, pp 311-318.

Gilmore R: 'A poor harvest; the clash of policies and interests in the grain trade', New York, Longman, 1982.

Goldin I and Knudsen O (Ed): 'Agricultural trade liberalization: implications for developing countries'. Paris, OECD Development Center, 1990.

Grigg D: 'The world food problem, 1950-1980'. Oxford, Basil Blackwell, 1985.

Grigsby S E and Arnade C A: 'The effect of exchange rate distortions on grain export markets: the case of Argentina', *American Journal of Agricultural Economics*, Vol 68, No 2, May 1986, pp 434-440.

Halbrendt C and Gempesaw C II: 'A policy analysis of China's wheat economy', *American Journal of Agricultural Economics*, Vol 72, No 2, May 1990, pp 268-278.

Harris S, Swinbank A and Wilkinson G: 'The food and farm policies of the European Community'. New York, John Wiley & Sons, 1983.

Hazell P: 'Sources of increased instability in world cereal production', *Journal of Agricultural Economics*, Vol 36, No 2, May 1985, pp 145-160.

Herrmann R: 'Agricultural price protection, import dependence and economic development: the case of wheat', *Journal of Agricultural Economics*, Vol 30, No 2, May 1989, pp 152-167.

Hopcraft P: 'Grain marketing policies and institutions in Africa', *Finance and Development*, March 1987, pp 37-40.

Ingco M: 'Changes in food consumption patterns in the Republic of Korea'. Washington DC, PRE Working Papers Series No 506, International Economics Department, The World Bank, September 1990.

International Monetary Fund: 'The CAP of the EC: principles and consequences'. Washington DC, IMF DM/88/1, 1988.

Kaynak E: 'World food marketing systems'. London, Butterworths, 1986.

Koester U: 'Policy options for the grain economy of the European Community: implications for developing countries'. Research Report #35, International Food Policy Research Institute, Washington DC, 1982.

Kuhn B, Shaviro F and Burke M: 'Market regulation and international use of futures markets', *American Journal of Agricultural Economics*, Vol 67, No 5, December 1985, pp 992-998.

Littmann E L: 'Agricultural policies in the USSR: problems, trends and prospects', *Journal of Agricultural Economics*, Vol 40, No 3, September 1989, pp 291-301.

Liu K and Roningen V O: 'The world grains-oilseeds-livestock (GOL) model: a simplified version'. Washington DC, Staff Report AGES850128, Economic Research Service, US Department of Agriculture, 1985.

MacBean L I and Nguyen D T: 'Commodity policies. Problems and prospects'. London, Croom Helm, 1987.

Malenbaum W: 'The world wheat economy 1885-1939'. Cambridge, Mass, Harvard University Press, 1953.

Marion B W: 'The organization and performance of the US food system'. Lexington Massachusetts, Lexington Books, 1986.

McDonald P, Edwards R A and Greenhalgh J F D: 'Animal nutrition.' 3rd edition, London, Longman, 1981.

Medvedev Z A: 'Soviet agriculture'. London and New York, W W Norton, 1987.

Mielke K D and de Gorter H: 'Impacts of the common agricultural policy on international wheat prices', *Journal of Agricultural Economics*, Vol 39, No 2, May 1988, pp 217-231.

Mitchell D O: 'A world grains and soybeans model'. Washington DC, Working Paper 1985-7, Commodity Studies and Projections Division, Economic and Research Staff, The World Bank, 1985.

Morgan D: 'Merchants of grain'. New York, Viking, 1979.

Nelson R D: 'Forward and futures contracts as pre-harvest commodity marketing instruments', *American Journal of Agricultural Economics*, Vol 67, No 1, February 1985, pp 15-23.

Paarlberg P L and Abbott P C: 'Oligopolistic behaviour of public agencies in international trade: the case of wheat', *American Journal of Agricultural Economics*, Vol 68, No 3, August 1986, pp 528-542.

Paarlberg P L and Sharples J A: 'Japanese and European Community agricultural trade policies: some US strategies'. Washington DC, United States Department of Agriculture, Economic Research Service, Foreign Agricultural Economic Report 204, 1984.

Paarlberg R: 'Lessons of the grain embargo', *Foreign Affairs*, Autumn 1980.

Paul A B, Heifner R G and Helmuth J W: 'Farmers' use of forward contracts and futures markets'. Washington DC, United States Department of Agriculture, National Economic Analysis Division, Economic Research Service, Agricultural Economics Report No 320, March 1976.

Petzel T: 'International use of US futures markets: discussion', *American Journal of Agricultural Economics*, Vol 67, No 5, December 1985, pp 999-1001.

Phillips P W G: 'Wheat, Europe and the GATT'. New York, St Martin's Press, 1990.

Raeburn J R: 'Agriculture: foundations, principles and development'. Chichester, John Wiley, 1984.

Rees G L: 'Britain's commodity markets'. London, Paul Elek Books, 1972.

Roberts I *et al*: 'US grain policies and the world market'. Canberra, Australian Bureau of Agricultural and Resource Economics, Policy Monograph No 4, 1989.

Runge, Ford C and Stanton G H: 'The political economy of the Uruguay Round negotiations: a view from Geneva', *American Journal of Agricultural Economics*, Vol 70, No 5, December 1988, pp 1146–1152.

Sarris A and Freebairn J W: 'Endogenous price policies and international wheat prices', *American Journal of Agricultural Economics*, Vol 65, No 2, May 1983, pp 214–224.

Schiff M: 'Information, expectations and policies: a study of the world wheat market'. Unpublished PhD thesis, University of Chicago, 1983.

Schiff M: 'An econometric analysis of the world wheat market and simulations of alternative policies'. Washington DC, US Department of Agriculture, Economic Research Service, 1985.

Sen A: 'Development strategies: the roles of the state and the private sector'. Proceedings of the World Bank Annual Conference of Development Economics 1990 (Contribution to a Roundtable Discussion), Supplement to the *World Bank Economic Review* and the *World Bank Research Observer*, Washington DC 1991.

Schmitz A: 'Agricultural trade liberalization and GATT: the Rolef Special Interest Groups', *American Journal of Agricultural Economics*, Vol 70, No 5, December 1988, pp 994–1005.

Shepherd G S and Futrell G A: 'Marketing farm products'. 7th edition, Ames, Iowa State University Press, 1982.

Singer H, Wood J and Jennings T: 'Food Aid, the challenge and the opportunity'. Oxford, Clarendon Press, 1987.

Streit M (Ed): 'Futures trading: modelling, managing and monitoring futures trading'. Oxford, Basil Blackwell, 1983.

Tang A and Stone B: 'Food production in the People's Republic of China'. Washington DC, International food policy research institute, May 1980.

Thompson S: 'Use of futures markets for exports by less developed countries', *American Journal of Agricultural Economics*, Vol 67, No 5, December 1985, pp 986–991

Tracy M: 'Agriculture in Western Europe'. 2nd edition, London, Granada, 1982.

Trager J: 'The great grain robbery'. New York, Ballantine, 1975.

Tsubota K: 'Agricultural policy in Japan', *Journal of Agricultural Economics*, Vol 36, No 3, September 1985, pp 363–376.

Tyers R and Anderson K: 'Liberalising OECD agricultural policies in the Uruguay Round: effects on trade and welfare', *Journal of Agricultural Economics*, Vol 39, No 2, May 1988, pp 197–216.

United States Bureau of the Census: 'Historical statistics of the United States: colonial times to 1970'. Washington DC, US Department of Commerce, 1975.

United States Bureau of the Census: 'Statistical abstract of the United States'. Washington DC, US Department of Commerce, annual.

United States Department of Agriculture, Foreign Agricultural Service: 'World grain situation and outlook'. Washington DC, monthly.

United States General Accounting Office: 'Agricultural trade: long term bilateral grain agreements with the Soviet Union and China'. Washington DC, General Accounting Office, Report GAO/NSIAD-89-63, 1989.

Veyne P: 'Bread and circuses'. Translated by Brian Pearce, London, Allen Lane, 1990.

Walters A: 'The economic consequences of agricultural support: a survey'. Paris, Organization for Economic Co-operation and Development, OECD Economic Studies, 9, 1987.

Wilson W, Koo W and Carter C A: 'Importer loyalty in the international wheat market', *Journal of Agricultural Economics*, Vol, 41, No 1, January 1990, pp 94-102.

World Bank: 'World development report 1991: the challenge of development'. Washington DC, World Bank, 1991.

Worldwatch Institute: 'State of the world 1990'. Washington DC, Worldwatch Institute, 1990.

Index